MODERN PSYCHOLOGY
in the ANCIENT BIBLE

ETHICAL MONOTHEISM IN THE HEBREW MIND

VICTOR M. ERLICH, PhD, MD

Charleston, SC
www.PalmettoPublishing.com

Modern Psychology in the Ancient Bible

First Edition

Hardcover ISBN: 978-1-68515-471-4
Paperback ISBN: 978-1-68515-470-7
eBook ISBN: 978-1-68515-472-1

And it shall come to pass, when many evils and troubles are befallen them, that this song shall testify against them as a witness . . . . for I know their imagination which they go about [i.e., *enact*] even now.

—Deuteronomy 31:21

For my esteemed psychiatrists:
Dr. Shala Erlich
Dr. Doron Raphaely
Dr. Joseph McCreery

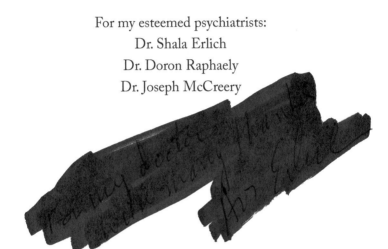

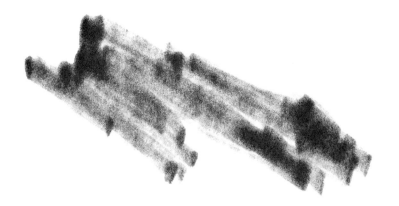

CONTENTS

INTRODUCTION
The Hebrew Bible and Psychology

I: The Hebrew Bible in the West's Literary Tradition

One does not expect to find modern psychological understanding in the Hebrew Bible, but there it is, woven into
the artfully composed narrative. The Hebrew Bible, the
Tanach, that ancient collection of the Torah, multiple books
of history and prophecy, as well as poetry, is not merely a
legal code, like that of Hammurabi, and not a philosoph-
ic discussion about the need for carefully-crafted laws, like
Plato's last dialogue, *The Laws*. Rather, the *Tanach*, within
its framework of divine provenance, partakes in the West's
longstanding literary tradition of artful narrative, from
the *Epic of Gilgamesh* (c. 2100 BCE) to the modern novel,

where characters possess minds and personalities, behaving accordingly, rationally or not.

That sacred Hebrew texts employ the language of men was the opinion of the Talmudic scholar, Rabbi Ishmael, who argued against the view of Rabbi Akiva, who claimed that sacred writings, especially the Torah, contained a unique, divinely-inspired language. But a bit of thoughtful reading of the *Tanach* shows that there is much truth in Rabbi Ishmael's point of view. For example, the opening of the *Iliad* begins by focusing on the wrath of Achilles and on the psychological roots of lust and warfare. So too, when Cain's sacrificial offering to God is inexplicably rejected, God asks Cain, "Why are you wroth?"

But there is a difference between Homer's and the *Tanach*'s interest in the psychological states of the characters they portray. Homer tells us that the wrath of Achilles is the result of meddling gods with conflicting goals, but when the text of Genesis, composed in the language of men, has God focus on Cain's feelings rather than on his heinous crime, the language of men brings us into the realm of the ancient Hebrews, actual human beings who had a particular need to understand why they thought and acted the way they did. Their very own perversity demanded a psychological explanation.

In my view, the multiple books of the *Tanach* focus specifically on why the Children of Israel found it so difficult to hold in their minds Abraham's covenant with an unseen God. One may have no interest in sacred covenants but still find value in the *Tanach*'s detailed presentation of the psychological difficulties involved in accepting any code of behavior, especially one rooted in deep, abstract thinking.

From beginning to end, the *Tanach* explores the psychology of those lapsed monotheists who escaped from the ethical burden of Mosaic Law to embrace beautiful women and their idolatrous gods. Even the wise Solomon, as we shall see, succumbed to the pursuit of gold and concubines, and was thus easily enticed to build idolatrous sites of worship to please the captivating Queen of Sheba.

By describing the mental lapses of legions of ancient Hebrews, starting with their fabrication the golden calf and concluding with a summary of the consequence of similar lapses, as set forth in the sublime Book of Lamentations, the authors of the *Tanach* thereby highlight the rich values of ethical monotheism and contrast it with its foolish-but-tempting alternatives.

My intention here is to demonstrate the depth of the *Tanach*'s understanding of psychology, both for its historical interest, and for its contribution to our modern understanding of why people choose rationally, or not. I hope that from my brief survey of the *Tanach* readers can obtain both a deeper understanding of the ancient Hebrews' artful view of themselves, as well as a useful summary of major issues in modern psychology.

Because questions of motivation and other psychological issues are often explored in the vast literature of the West, I will occasionally allude to parallels between the *Tanach* and secular literature, which borrows from the Hebrews more often than the other way around. In *Moby Dick*, for example, Herman Melville borrows heavily from the biblical study of Ahab and Jezebel. Shakespeare himself alludes in *Hamlet* to details in the story of King David's conniving murder of Uriah.

The ancient Hebrews were particularly in need of a psychology that could explain the differences between their beliefs and the beliefs of their neighbors. Worshippers of the god Ba'al Peor favored child sacrifice, but the Hebrews did not, at least not most of the time. At other times the Hebrews were ambivalent about idolatrous practices, leaning this way and that, as did those standing before Elijah on Mount Carmel. But often the stubborn Hebrews were drawn into the very depths of idolatry, thus provoking beautifully-crafted prophecies of rebuke.

The Hebrews slowly came to believe that they needed a psychological explanation for their erratic embrace of ethical monotheism, as well as an explanation for the behavior of their grossly irrational neighbors, whom they often admired. What, after all, leads one to choose ethical monotheism rather than the rites of Molech, the fire god? Why should one value the one and not the other?

To answer these questions the *Tanach* undertakes a psychological examination of a large cast of characters, from the mythical Adam and Eve, Cain and Noah, on through the fabled heroes of the Bible, Samson, Saul, David, and Solomon, and then into the Hebrew Bible's canonically-labeled literary work, which includes David's Psalms, Hosea's salacious prophecies, Solomon's erotic Song of Songs, and Jeremiah's elegiac Lamentations. The *Tanach*, like the great literary works of the West, follows a thematic thread as it inquires into the kind of mind that can value monotheism.

How do monotheists evaluate what is rational and what is irrational, and how do they choose the most life-enhancing way to govern their lives? The Hebrews' answers to these questions might be of little interest to a modern reader, but their psychological thoughts, delivered by beautifully-crafted stories, are worth consideration, if only as a foundation for a better understanding of human motivation.

CHAPTER ONE
Cain: Cognition and Impulse

In modern neurology we recognize that the human brain's capacity for cognition is largely localized in the frontal lobes, which are much larger in human brains compared to the brains of other primates. Our frontal cortices, beginning just behind our foreheads and reaching back to our ears, are widely connected to other parts of our brains, so that we may weave all aspects of a current challenge into a coherent plan, one that is more likely to succeed than an impulsive act based on raw emotion.

Those raw emotions are managed in the limbic system, a bilateral, circular structure that runs deep below our cognitive cortices, from the amygdala in the anterior temporal lobe to the posterior brain, then circles frontally through the cingulate gyrus to the hypothalamic nucleus, and then back to the amygdala:

The Limbic System

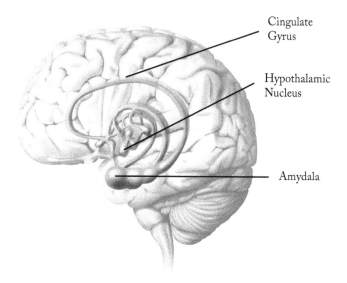

Cingulate
Gyrus

Hypothalamic
Nucleus

Amydala

Rational behavior depends on the frontal lobe's ability to consider all factors related to the constantly shifting inputs of experience. A well-honed executive function permits an integration of all the relevant factors of the moment, thus taming an otherwise unbridled limbic system. This view provides an anatomic foundation for Freud's abstract idea of the ego and the id; the ego is the product of the cognitive apparatus in the frontal lobes, and the more primitive limbic system drives the id's wild passions.

Cognitive capacity and primitive drives are inevitably in conflict in the human mind, as the poets have long known. In Christopher Marlowe's *Dr. Faustus*, for example, the bedeviled doctor sees a vision of the famous beauty, Helen, and asks:

> Was this the face that launch'd a thousand ships,
> And burnt the topless towers of Ilium—
> Sweet Helen, make me immortal with a kiss."

The human mind's pursuit of both "a kiss" and blood-thirsty violence is illustrated both in the *Iliad*, and, uncannily, in the story of Cain's murder of his innocent brother, Abel. Cain's fratricide is surprisingly followed by the story of Cain's descendants becoming makers of tools and musical instruments. Thus "the mark of Cain" did not brand Cain for divine punishment, as is often thought, but protected him from the fatal lot of those strangers in the ancient world who had been banished from their native lands because of criminality.

But Cain was not merely a criminal. He had to be protected because he was also a normal human being. He must live, so that he might master his violent proclivities. In the King-James translation (which I use because of its superb mastery of Elizabethan prose), the story of Cain, a tiller, and his younger brother Abel, a shepherd, goes like this in Genesis 4:3-8:

Cain brought of the fruit of the ground an offering unto the Lord . . . . And Abel, he also brought of the firstlings of his flock and of the fat thereof. And the Lord had respect unto Abel and his offering. But unto Cain and of his offering He had no respect. And Cain was very wroth, and his countenance fell. And the Lord said unto Cain, Why art thou wroth? and why is thy countenance fallen? If thou doest well, shalt though not be accepted? and if thou doest not well, sin lieth at the door. And unto thee shall be his desire, and thou shalt rule over him. And Cain talked with Able his brother: and it came to pass, when they were in the field, that Cain rose up against Abel his brother, and slew him.

The Lord makes it clear that Cain is himself responsible for his fury. Yes, the King-James translators draw on the longstanding belief that an external demon can lie in wait for a potential sinner and then invade and corrupt his mind, like the one here named "Sin." Versions of lurking devils commonly appeared in the folklore of the ancient Middle East and have remained in common belief today in many other habitations to which the devils have migrated.

But the Ancient Hebrews eschewed all this nonsense, recognizing it as a form of idolatry, as in Deuteronomy, 18:9-13:

When thou art come into the land which the Lord thy God giveth thee, thou shalt not learn to do after the abominations of those nations. There

shall not be found among you any one that maketh
his son or his daughter pass through the fire, one
who practices divinations, an astrologer, . . . an
enchanter, or a witch or a charmer, or a consulter
with familiar spirits, or a wizard, or a necromancer. For all that do such things are an abomination unto the Lord . . . Thou shalt be perfect
[*tamim* = complete, the adjective in Genesis 25:27
applied to Jacob to distinguish him from Esau, the
wild hunter].

Though the Hebrew God was the Creator of all things,
He Himself did not create witches, wizards or necroman-
cers; these forbidden goblins must be phantasmagorical creations of idolatrous minds. Because the Hebrews believed
themselves to be created in the image of a rational Creator,
they should be "perfect," like Jacob, in banning all forms of
mental folly.

Lacking a sophisticated psychology, they could not
definitively locate irrational folly in the human mind itself.
Sometimes, the best they could do was to assign evil proclivities to God Himself, as in I Samuel 16:14, where the
source of King Saul's tormented psychology is God:

The Spirit of the Lord departed from Saul, and
an evil spirit from the Lord troubled him."

But just as the story of Saul eventually locates his madness in the King's own mind, as we shall soon see, so too
does the story of Cain focus our attention on his responsibility for his acts.

By preferring Abel's sacrifice for no obvious reason, the Lord may have triggered Cain's uncontrollable fury, but fratricide was located in Cain's own mind, where no devils lurked. Eventually, the ancient Hebrews came to understand that they were in charge of their own minds, a Chosen People only in the sense that they were chosen to choose. Each Hebrew had to choose between the rival inclinations of his or her own mind. One could choose irrational idolatry or rational monotheism. Thus a major theme of the *Tanach* is the contrast between that which is rational and that which is not. As we shall see, this led to a psychological exploration into the nature of mind.

But for now, let us go back to Cain. He is *not* portrayed as a maniac invaded by a homicidal demon. Rather, the Torah shows Cain to be a typical man whose conflicted mind hosts both a creative spirit and an impulsive limbic system, often prone to violence. In the Hebrew text, there is no hint of an external demon haunting Cain, and there is no "door" through which this imaginary devil might enter. The Hebrew word *petach* means "opening," not "door," and the "opening" here is not meant literally.

God is careful to remind Cain that he alone is responsible for having chosen his own murderous impulses. If he gets a hold of himself, God tells him, he will be "accepted," and if he doesn't control himself, God will again withdraw from him. God does not warn Cain about prowling demons, but instead alerts Cain to his own bestial passions. The Hebrew verb in the phrase "Sin lieth at the door" is *rovetz*, which means "prowls like a beast," and in this context, the beast can only be Cain's irascible drives. Nobody but God has entered Cain's mind, and what He finds there has always been there, for God created Cain with intra-psychic conflict, in just the way He created the entire line of Adam. Those who defensively claim "The Devil made me do it," have not learned the lessons that the *Tanach* has taught the Children of Israel.

Though he is said to have lived long before Moses, Cain was put in the Torah to choose to follow the laws of ethical monotheism, or, alternatively, to follow his primitive drives. This responsibility to choose rationality is formally laid out in Deuteronomy 11:26-29, where God asks the Hebrews to chose between rational monotheistic values, as represented by Mount Gerizim, and irrational idolatry, represented by Mount Ebal.

> Behold, I set before you this day a blessing and a curse: A blessing if ye obey the commandments of the Lord your God . . . . And a curse if ye . . . turn aside out of the way . . . to go after other gods which ye have not known. . . . Thou shalt put the blessing upon mount Gerizim, and the curse upon mount Ebal.

God's Chosen People are chosen to choose between two distinct states of mind. And Cain is indeed of two minds. A seemingly superfluous phrase, related to Cain's cognitive capacity, is artfully placed as a prelude to his brutish act of murder:

> And Cain talked with Abel his brother, and it
> came to pass, when they were in the field, that Cain
> rose up against Abel his brother, and slew him.

Cain first expresses his cognitive self as he "talked with Abel his brother," presumably about the work lying before them, the one as a tiller and the other as a shepherd "in the field"; then in a flash Cain succumbs to his wild id.

The story goes on in Genesis 4 to enumerate Cain's (and his descendants') creative skills. Though he is now remembered for murdering his brother, Cain has another side. The Lord marks him for protection because he and his kin must survive, so that civilization will arise, along with husbandry, metallurgy, and music, thus endowing mankind with sufficient understanding to choose creatively and rationally, thereby becoming capable of founding humane civilizations:

> Therefore whosoever slayeth Cain, vengeance
> shall be taken on him sevenfold. And the Lord set
> a mark upon Cain, lest any finding him should kill
> him. And Cain went out from the presence of the
> Lord . . . . And Cain knew his wife; and she con-
> ceived, and bare Enoch: and he builded a city . . . .
> [And] Jabal was the father of such as dwell in tents
> and of such as have cattle. And his brother's name
> was Jubal: . . . the father of all such as handle the
> harp and organ . . . . And Tubal-Cain [carries the
> name of his ancestor and is] an instructor of every
> artificer in brass and iron.

This old fable of Cain and Abel can thus be read as serious social psychology, whether or not one believes in God, or in anything else. For a civilization of ethical human beings to thrive, a well-developed ego, armed with reason and creativity, must triumph over the irascible id, thereby opening opportunities for those who build civilized cities, and for "every artificer in brass and iron."

Apparently Wordsworth and Coleridge were alert to this meaning of the biblical story. While enjoying one of their famous strolls in the Lake District, they sketched out a joint plan to compose a poem about Cain and his first descendent, Enoch, as they too took a stroll through imaginary woods. This holiday project foundered, with Wordsworth producing nothing. But Coleridge composed a few lines about Cain and Enoch (*Enos*, to Coleridge), called "The Wanderings of Cain":

> "It is dark, O my father!" said Enos, "but the path under our feet is smooth and soft, and we shall soon come out into the open moonlight."
>
> And Cain lifted up his voice and cried bitterly, and said, "The Mighty One that persecuteth me is on this side and on that; he pursueth my soul like the wind; . . . . I desire to die—yea, the things that never had life, ... seem precious to mine eyes. O that a man might live without the breath of his nostrils. So I might abide in darkness, and blackness, and an empty space! Yea, I would lie down, I would not rise. . . . Then Enos spake to his father, "Arise my father, arise" . . . Then the child took

> hold of his father, as if he would raise him: and Cain being faint and feeble rose slowly on his knees and pressed himself against the trunk of a fir, and stood upright and followed the child.

Coleridge catches the "dark" psychology of repentant Cain, the humane kindness of Enoch, and the creativity of both father and son in their elegiac language. That Coleridge and Wordsworth could see value in the line of fratricidal Cain corroborates the *Tanach*'s demonstration that rational creativity can overcome primitive drives. One might note in passing that Freud's third agency of mind, the superego, that harshly critical supervisor of the ego, is a superfluous idea in the perspectives of both the *Tanach* and Coleridge, which already accommodate the cultivated mind's capacity to manage harsh self-criticism, its longing for "darkness, and blackness, and empty space."

The Hebrews were probably the first civilization to distinguish rational psychology from irrationality, though the Greeks came close. Making a sharp distinction between irrational idolatry and rational monotheism was more important to the Hebrews than to the Greeks, who maintained a proper obeisance to the whims of local gods. Even Socrates praised the Greek gods who, in league with blinkered Athenian judges, condemned him to an unjust death. Because the Hebrews believed that their God and His Laws were rational, they were forced to explore how the mind integrates competing demands to produce rational behavior, or its opposite. I focus on this exploration throughout, especially in Chapter Six's examination of Samson's impaired executive function, and in Chapter Twelve's study of how the *Tanach* grapples with the idea of reason itself.

CHAPTER TWO
THE STUDY OF PERCEPTION

I: HANNAH IS MISPERCEIVED

The study of how human beings assemble the external world in their minds provided the foundation of modern psychology. After neuropsychologists achieved a rudimentary understanding of the pathways from our organs of sense to the brain, they went on to study how we use our mental representations to produce ideas, some better than others. Over millennia of astute observation by poets and perceptive thinkers, and then by formal psychologists, we now have some understanding of how we see what we see and how we work with what we have perceived.

That any of this accumulated knowledge appears in the ancient Hebrew Bible is somewhat surprising, but a knowing eye can see that the *Tanach* pays careful attention to how we interpret what we perceive.

The ancient Hebrew's simple epistemology divided reasoning into two categories, the rational and the irrational, the latter represented by idolatry of all kinds, and the former by their own monotheistic ethics. They thus devoted a good deal of effort to distinguish the one from the other. This effort often appears in tangential details, unrelated to the story line, but nevertheless relevant to the underlying question of why people believe what they think they see. This quiet effort to understand perception is worth our consideration, as psychologists are still exploring how we construct what we think we know.

A good example of the *Tanach*'s effort to understand perception is found in the first chapter of I Samuel, where we are told how Samuel came to be born, which was of course necessary for him to become the first Judge of Israel, but not obviously important to the story of his career. This story has more to do with human perception than it does with Samuel the Judge. We find in this story three examples of misinterpretation of accurately observed perceptions, followed by an example of plain misperception:

> Now there was a certain man . . . and his name was Elkanah . . . . And he had two wives; the name of the one was Hannah, and the name of the other Peninnah; and Peninnah had children, but Hannah had no children . . . . And . . . Elkanah . . . gave to Peninnah his wife, and to all her sons and

her daughters portions: But unto Hannah he gave
a worthy portion [Hebrew *manah achat apayim* =
double portion]; for he loved Hannah: but the Lord
had shut up her womb. And her adversary [Penin-
nah] also provoked her sore, because the Lord had
shut up her womb . . . therefore she wept, and
did not eat. Then said Elkanah her husband to her,
Hannah, why weepest thou? And why eatest thou
not? And why is thy heart grieved? Am I not better
than ten sons?

Because this seems a mere overture to the main story
of Hannah becoming pregnant with her son, Samuel, not
many readers pause to notice Elkanah's inability to interpret
the meaning of what he sees and hears from his despondent
wife, Hannah. Yes, he registers that she weeps and doesn't
eat, but he finds this so puzzling that he has to guess its
explanation, and he guesses incorrectly. Hannah's sorrow
is *not* mitigated by receiving Elkanah's double portions, nor
does she care if Elkanah thinks that he is "better than ten
sons."

Rather, motivated by maternal needs, she obviously longs for a child, a hope that is intensified by her rival
having borne many children. Peninnah, too, misinterprets
Hannah's weeping and fasting, but in a different way. For
this other wife, this other sensibility, Hannah's grief is not
pitiable but an invitation to pile on more torment.

Bereft of fertility, understanding, and compassion, Hannah flees to the Temple in Jerusalem, to Eli, the High Priest.

There she receives the blessing she seeks, but not before Eli realizes that he can't see straight:

> And she was in bitterness of soul, and prayed unto the Lord, and wept sore. And she vowed a vow, and said, O Lord of hosts, if thou wilt indeed look on the affliction of thine handmaid, and remember me, . . . but will give unto thine handmaid a man child, then I will give him unto the Lord all the days of his life, and there shall no razor come upon his head. And it came to pass, as she continued praying before the Lord, that Eli marked her mouth. Now Hannah, she spake in her heart; only her lips moved, but her voice was not heard; therefore Eli thought she had been drunken. And Eli said unto her, How long wilt thou be drunken? put away thy wine from thee. And Hannah answered and said, No my lord, I am a woman of a sorrowful spirit: I have drunk neither wine nor strong spirit, but have poured out my soul before the Lord. Count not thine handmaid for a daughter of Belial, for out of the abundance of my complaint and grief have I spoken hitherto.

Though Eli immediately blunders as he sizes up the woman mumbling before him, his mis-perception is easily corrected. After hearing Hannah's rational explanation, he quickly recognizes that what he saw as plain as day, Hannah's silent moving of her lips, led him to misjudge the pious lady; he thought her drunk. But after receiving a rational explanation, he reorients himself appropriately. His error would have been much more problematic if he were incapable of seeing that he had misperceived.

Realizing that the capacity to perceive accurately and interpret correctly permits one to distinguish the rational from the irrational, the ancient Hebrew writers entered more deeply into the nature of human perception, which led them to remarkably modern insights.

II: Some Spies See and Some Don't

Subjectivity is extensively explored in modern psychology's investigation of human perception, including studies of optical illusions, false memories of things never seen, mis-identifications of supposed criminals in police line-ups, and mis-interpretations of supposedly scientific experiments. What we think we saw, and what we think these phantoms mean, often compose beliefs that fail to pass objective inspection.

The ancient Hebrews understood this long before the field of psychology existed. Whether we believe that the Five Books of Moses were composed by God or by human beings, we see that the Promised Land was perceived differently, depending on the perceiver. The Torah demands an understanding of why some of those were sent to explore the Land people evaluated what they saw in a rational way and some otherwise, raising the question of how one might distinguish a rational system of perception from its opposite.

Four centuries ago, Sir Francis Bacon, in *The Advancement of Learning*, distinguished four types of "*Idols*" (a term Sir Francis borrowed from the *Tanach*) that keep men from advancing learning. These idols are not things but abstractions for ideas that mislead the mind. The Torah compacts Bacon's four idols into a single, abstract idea called idolatry, *avoda zara, "strange worship,"* which diverts thought into the realm of ignorance.

That the ancient Hebrews diligently sought to differentiate rational perception from an idolatrous point of view is clearly seen Numbers 13, where Moses sends spies from their temporary encampment in Sinai into the Land of Canaan. These twelve, one from each of the twelve tribes of Israel, constitute a representative sample of the national mindset, a surprisingly modern kind of survey. We would expect this inquiry to reveal how grateful these former slaves were to receive a divine gift of their own Land

We would also expect that the results of this survey to be heavily positive, for why wouldn't they be?

But we learn that only two of the twelve perceived the divine value of the Promised Land, while the other ten saw nothing of abstract value, only terrifying giants and material things that they could taste, enjoy, and haul.

This is what these recent escapees from slavery had to say about what they thought they saw in the Promised Land:

And they returned from searching of the land after forty days. And they went and came to Moses,

and to Aaron, and to all the congregation of the
children of Israel . . . and brought back word
unto them . . . and shewed them the fruit of the
land. And they . . . said, We came unto the land
wither thou sentest us, and surely it floweth with
milk and honey; and this is the fruit of it. Nevertheless the people be strong that dwell in the land, and
the cities are walled, and very great: and moreover
we saw the children of Anak [Giants] there. The
Amalekites dwell in the land to the south; and the
Hittites and the Jebusites, and the Amorites. And
the Cananites dwell by the sea . . . . And Caleb
stilled the people before Moses, and said, Let us go
up at once and possess it; for we are well able to
overcome it. But the men that went up with him
said, We be not able to go up against the people; for
they are stronger than we. And they brought up an
evil report of the land . . . saying, The land . . . is
a land that eateth up the inhabitants thereof; and
all the people we saw in it are men of great stature. And there we saw the giants, the sons of Anak,
which come of giants: and we were in our own sight
as grasshoppers, and so we were in their sight.

The challenge that Caleb sees as manageable, the other spies see as insurmountable. These conflicting points of
view go deeper than common subjectivity, for the self-di-
minishing spies assume that the giants they fear would
agree that they are as puny as grasshoppers. Modern psychologists would likely note that these frightened spies were
off-loading their sense of puniness by projecting it into the

imagined perceptions of their idolatrous enemies, the very people whose irrational thinking the Hebrews were meant to replace.

This view that the Amalekites are unconquerable contrasts sharply with how the Hebrews previously perceived the Amalekite threat. With the help of their Lord, they easily defeated these cowardly enemies who attacked the weakest stragglers in the rear of the Hebrew procession through the hot desert. The pessimistic spies even forgot that the Lord commanded them to preserve the story of their earlier mastery of the Amalekites. They were to *remember to forget* the Amalekites. In Chapters 4 and 15, we will come back to this complex command to remember to blot out the memory of a defeated people, but here let us note that the majority of these spies who once easily defeated the Amalekites now perceive them as undefeatable. This story of subjective, conflicting reports about the nature of the Hebrew national home likely finds a place in the Torah to remind the stiff-necked Hebrews that their inability to perceive and interpret accurately would continue to hobble their pursuit of a rational and pious life.

Reminders could not of course help the Hebrews' neighbors, who did not have the capacity to doubt their irrational beliefs, such as the necessity to sacrifice their children to their fire god, Molech (a cognate of Hebrew *melech*, king). Only those who seek a rational and just society can take advantage of a story about their own tendency to mis-perceive.

The spies' misperception immediately produces a chain reaction. After hearing the shocking description of the Promised Land, the congregation immediately responds in kind:

> And all the congregation lifted up their voice, and cried; and the people wept that night. And all the children of Israel murmured against Moses and against Aaron: . . . Would God that we had died in the Land of Egypt! Or would God we had died in the wilderness! And wherefore hath the Lord brought us unto this land to fall by the sword, that our wives and our children should be a prey? Were it not better for us to return unto Egypt. And they said one to the other, Let us make a captain, and let us return into Egypt. Then Moses and Aaron fell onto their faces before all of the assembly . . . . And Joshua the son of Nun, and Caleb . . . . rent their clothes: And they spake unto all the company . . . saying, The land which we passed through to search it, is an exceeding good land. If the Lord delight in us, then he will bring us into the land and give it us; a land which floweth with milk and honey. Only rebel not ye against the Lord, neither fear ye the people of the land; for they are bread for us: their defense is departed from them and the Lord is with us: fear them not. But all the congregation bade stone them with stones.

There is an implied question here. Should this land be granted to a people claiming that they will use the land as an emblem of an ethical way of life, or should the land be left in the hands of child-sacrificing idolaters? One is not required to believe that the Hebrews' invisible God has the privilege to give away land to newcomers. Rather one is invited to consider this specifically Hebrew question in the light of ancient Hebrew civilization.

Are Moses' stiff-necked Hebrews able to perceive the emblematic value of the Land they have been promised by an abstract God, in the manner of Caleb and Joshua? Or is their understanding blunted, in the manner of the other spies' false perception of an unconquerable land full of terrifying giants? Might the minds of the stiff-necked Hebrews rise to an understanding of Mosaic values, or will they sink back into the dumbness of stones?

Trapped by their warped perspective, the skeptical spies are indeed driven to stones in the sense that they wish to stone Moses and Aaron for preventing them from going back to slavery in Egypt! To overcome this kind of madness requires a deep understanding of how our interpretations of what we think we have perceived shape our choices.

Based on their perverse understanding, the weaker-minded spies ask, in effect, "Might we not do better as slaves than chasing this invisible God through a howling desert?"

A rough outline of a better understanding of the value of the Promised Land is given promptly in Numbers 15. Instead of giving a home to idolatrous worshippers who sacrifice their children to Molech, the Land was to represent the devotion to one God, one system of justice, and one road to rationality. This requires an honest inquiry into the mental capacities needed to create a rational and just society, rather than an unreasonable belief in any particular religion:

> And the priest shall make an atonement for the soul that sinneth ignorantly, when he sinneth by ignorance before the Lord, to make an atonement for him; and it shall be forgiven him. Ye shall have one law for him that sinneth through ignorance, both for him that is both among the children of Israel, and for the stranger that sojourneth among them. But for the soul that doeth ought presumptuously, whether he be born in the land or a stranger, . . . Because he hath despised the word of the Lord, and hath broken his commandment, that soul shall utterly be cut off.

The Hebrews knew that each of their idolatrous neighbors followed the dictates of their own gods, with each god denying the legitimacy of all the others. Because each of these legislating gods were themselves irrational animals or manmade objects, not even one of these idolatrous lawmakers could be rational. The Hebrews believed that a rational and just system of law must be applied equally to all citizens, "whether born in the land or a stranger," an idea that can be accepted only by a society that is devoted to a single, just God.

When that God commands that the Hebrews to pursue justice, as in Deuteronomy 16.20, He emphasizes that justice is not an objective thing, but an idea based on one's perspective:

> Judges . . . shalt thou make thee in all thy gaits, which the Lord thy God giveth thee, . . . and they shall judge the people with just [Hebrew *tsedek*] judgment Thou shall not wrest judgment; thou shall not respect persons [i.e. favor the rich], neither take a gift: for a gift doth blind the eyes of the wise, and pervert the words of the righteous [Hebrew *tsadikim*, "the Just"]. That which is alto-gether-just [Hebrew *tsedek-tsedek*, "justice doubled, absolutely just"] shalt thou follow, that thou mayest live and inherit the land which the Lord thy God giveth thee.

In the original Hebrew, the root *tsedek* appears here in several words related to the ideas of justice, *just*, *altogether just*, *righteous*, and *the just*. The King-James translators, giv-en the nature of English, had to be satisfied with a variety of English roots to capture what is, in Hebrew, a unified idea. Under the canopy of a single, invisible but rational God, *justice* is a single, abstract idea whose value depends on the perspicacity of those who are urged to be just, even abso-lutely just. Only those who can see the values that the land represents will "live and inherit the land which the Lord thy God giveth." Those who are blind to these values will not survive long, which was to be the fate of both the idolatrous Canaanites and the blind spies.

To administer the Law justly in the Promised Land was no easy task. One must not favor the rich or the poor but focus on a just interpretation of each particular case's details, free of bribes and bias, and careful to root out perjury. In Exodus 23:1-3, we see another announcement that a successful life in the Promised Land depends on a righteous perspective, free from corrupting influences:

> Thou shall not raise a false report: put not thy hand with the wicked to be an unrighteous witness, . . . neither shalt thou speak in a cause to . . . wrest judgment. Neither shall thou countenance a poor man in his cause [Hebrew *v'dal lo tehader b're-bo*, do not favor a poor man in his case]. . . . Keep thee far from a false matter . . . . And thou shalt take no gift; for the gift blindeth the wise, and perverteth the words of the righteous. . . . Also thou shalt not oppress a stranger: for ye know the heart of a stranger, seeing ye were strangers in the land of Egypt.

God Himself tells the Hebrews that an unbiased perspective leads to appropriate judgment and justice in general. The misperceiving spies are thus not equipped to follow ethical monotheism, for which the Land is an emblem (see Avi Erlich, *Ancient Zionism*).

After the slandering spies die of a plague foisted on them as a punishment for their ignorant rejection of the Promised Land, their sympathizers mourn appropriately, and then foolishly decide to take another run at surveying

the Promised Land. Moses, knowing the perverse minds
of these men, tries stopping their ill-conceived plan by
reminding them that the Lord no longer supports their mission, likely because these spies are unable to see clearly. Of
course, Moses' warning is of no avail:

> And they rose up early in the morning, and
> they gat them up to the mountain, saying, Lo, we
> be here, and will go up unto the place which the
> Lord hath promised: for we have sinned. And
> Moses said, Wherefore do ye transgress the com-
> mandment of the Lord? But it shall not prosper.
> Go not up, for the Lord is not among you . . .
> For the Amalekites and the Canaanites are there
> before you, and ye shall fall by the sword: because
> ye have turned away from the Lord, therefore the
> Lord will not be with you. But they presumed to
> go up unto the hilltop . . . . Then the Amalekites
> came down, and the Canaanites which dwelt in that
> hill, and smote them, even unto Hormah [Hebrew
> *Ha-Kharma*, "The Annihilation"].

The meaning of the name of the place to which the
blind spies were driven for their final slaying provides a
warning about the danger of inadequate perception and its
consequent inadequate understanding.

From the time of Abraham, The Land of Israel represented more than the material home of the Hebrews. More
importantly, it represented an idea, a covenant between a
unique God and his devoted people to establish a just and

rational society, free of irrational idolatry. In the Hebrew view, a just and rational society can be created only for a people governed by a consistent set of laws that are applied equally to all and inspired by a single Creator who demands uncorrupted justice.

This Kantian worldview, this way of seeking unity, this distinction between coherence and chaos, can be admired independently of the Bible from which it is derived. For on this view rests every humane civilization that has survived on this globe. That is, any people aspiring to live well will commit themselves to the idea, which is also a blessing, that they are one nation under a rational God, with liberty and justice for all.

CHAPTER THREE
DELUSION

I: THE PSYCHOLOGY OF DELUSION

That human beings, even those of great intelligence, often act on delusory beliefs was well-recognized in the ancient world, though not in a psychological sense. For if a man were deluded during the Golden Age of Greece, the cause did not arise from his own mind but from the machinations of one or another meddling god. Such was the case with Paris, who was so deluded by the value of possessing the beautiful Helen, the wife of Menelaus, that he recklessly snatched her away to his home in Troy, bringing down on him and his fellow Trojans a sorrowful defeat. The fault for this disaster, however, was not innate in Paris' mind. Rather, the instigation of mayhem lay with the gods. The goddess of Delusion and Ruin, *Até*, guaranteed that deluded men suffer irreparably, as Aeschylus tells us in his tragedy, *Agamemnon* (355-361):

> Upon his [the delusional man's] people he brings a taint against which there is no defense; no god listens to his prayers. The man associated with such a deed, him they destroy in his unrighteousness. Such was Paris, who came to the house . . . of [Menelaus] and dishonored the hospitality of his host by stealing away a wedded wife [Helen].

But this was obviously too narrow a view to explain the fantastical variety of delusional thoughts of human beings, and it was without any anatomic foundation.

Without a clear understanding of the neuroanatomical basis of any of the several types of delusion, we must settle for Karl Jaspers' general definition, offered in 1959 solely on the basis of observed phenomenology. A delusion, says Dr. Jaspers, is a perverted view of reality that is not amenable to logic, and though the absurdity of this view is manifest to others, the patient, otherwise intelligent, cannot perceive any error in his bizarre convictions.

The ancient Hebrews could not achieve Jaspers' clarity, but they did manage to portray in stories the delusional mind in a way that resembles Jaspers' reliance on observation. The *Tanach* presents delusional Hebrews pursuing foreign women and their foreign gods even while they demonstrate many complex skills required by nation building. Most rational readers can see from the facts presented the clear irrationality of the blind Hebrews, who could not themselves see anything problematic with their attraction to the sex goddess, Ashtoreth, and the fire god, Molech.

Perhaps the most striking example of the Hebrews' delusional enthusiasm for idolatrous worship comes in poignant poetry by the minor prophet, Hosea. Like the ancient Greeks, Hosea lacks sufficient science to support his views, forcing him to turn to poetry in order to elucidate the nature of delusion.

Hosea sets his scene just before the destruction of the Northern Kingdom of Israel and the consequent loss of ten of the original twelve tribes of Israel. The leader of these lost tribes at that time seems to have been Ephraim, who led the easily corruptible Hebrews to embrace Ba'al (a general name for lords of this and that, like Beelzebub, the Lord of the Flies). And they pursued Ba'al so intensely, so lasciviously, that Hosea presents his countrymen as sex-maniacs chasing after whores. The prophet even intensifies his indictment by claiming the he himself had married a harlot, following a recommendation of the Lord Himself. The Lord seems to have been ironical here, insinuating that Hosea will have to marry a whore because there are no righteous brides remaining in the brave new Land of whoredom:

And the Lord said to Hosea, Go, take thee a wife of whoredoms and the children of whoredoms: for the land hath committed great whoredom, departing from the Lord.

Hosea does marry exactly as the Lord commands, with the expected results. The repetition here of the word *whoredom* three times is sufficient to alert us to the spiritual kind of whoredom about which we are reading (and Hosea continues to repeat the word later on in this prophetic poem). In this realm of an extended metaphor, the Children of Israel are the unfaithful wife of the Lord, who is not pleased by the behavior of his harlot/wife/people. He begs the few righteous children of the harlot to confront their mother, as in Hosea 2:2-3:

> Plead with your mother, plead: for she is not my wife, neither am I her husband: let her therefore put away her whoredoms out of her sight, and her adulteries from between her breasts; Lest I strip her naked, and set her as in the day that was born, . . . and make her a wilderness and set her like a dry land, and slay her with thirst.

Hosea's salacious, hyperbolic language seems appropriate only in serving as a measure of the intensity of the Hebrews' devotion to Ba'al. Does this not capture Jaspers' definition of delusion as a belief system that is intense, resistant to logic, and unassailable by rational doubters?

Hosea continues to present the erotic pleasure that the Hebrews bring to their embrace of Ba'al. For after all, Ba'al means not only lord, but husband. The erotic passion for Ba'al is represented as an untreatable delusion. Even the

Lord cannot undo the Hebrews' sexualized madness, though He does try, as we go on with Hosea's prophecy:

> And I will not have mercy on her children: for they be the children of whoredoms. For their mother hath played the harlot: . . . for she said, I will go after my lovers, that give me my bread and my water, my wool, my oil and my drink.

Here the skilled narrator alludes to God's promise to supply the very amenities that Hosea's whorish Hebrews assume will be better supplied by Ba'al. Of course, the God of Israel offered these amenities on condition that his people cleave to His rational system of law, as set forth in Deuteronomy 11:13-14:

> And it shall come to pass, if ye shall hearken diligently unto my commandments, which I command you this day, to love the Lord thy God, . . . That I will give you the rain of your land in due season, . . . That thou mayest gather in thy corn, and thy wine, and thy oil.

Hosea thus means his readers to understand that his whorish people have indeed replaced their rational Lord with a preferable lord, the all-sustaining Ba'al, the rain-maker, the guarantor of crops. Even if modern readers are indifferent about which imaginary god is more likely to be the best provider, they might be interested in a system of belief that is likely to sustain an enduring people. By having his whorish Hebrews turn to Ba'al for the same sustenance offered by their rational and pious God, Hosea is able to test, in a primitive way to be sure, whether all beliefs are equally delusional.

Hosea demonstrates how far from a just and life-affirming system of belief the former slaves have wandered. In embracing their new god, Ba'al, they have entangled themselves in a dangerous, almost comical system of belief, as they practice their new religion. Because the original Hebrew is more vivid and more telling, I will amend just a bit the King-James version of Hosea 13:1-2:

> And now they sin more and more and have made them molten images of their silver, and idols according to their own understanding, all of it the work of craftsmen: they say of them [the idols], Let the men that sacrifice kiss the calves [better translated as "They who sacrifice a man may kiss calves"].

The mistranslation of the original Hebrew arises from the translators' ignorance of a peculiarity of Hebrew grammar. Hebrew has its own way of indicating the genitive case. One does not say in Hebrew "The children of Israel." Rather, one uses a special form of the noun *children* that means "the children of," which is then placed immediately before the noun *Israel* to render "the Children of Israel" in two words, *b'nai yisrael*. Similarly, the correct translation of the last part of Hosea 13:2 is as indicated above.

Thus, in the Egyptian and Canaanite world of human sacrifice, being able to kiss calves is an appropriate reward for sacrificing a human being, especially a child (Apis, the bull god, along with his bull calves, were commonly worshipped in Egypt and the ancient Levant).

Of course, being rewarded for performing child sacrifice is terrifyingly absurd. But Hosea's intention is not to terrify but to educate the stiff-necked Hebrews about the danger of delusional thinking. He does this in two ways. One is by using a surprisingly modern medical approach, which requires a careful clinical history, thus showing the disease in action. The second aspect of Hosea's methodology is his artful use of metaphor, allusion, and drama. Without a scientific psychology, Hosea drew on his own creativity, apparently believing that he was created in his Creator's image.

In his conclusion, Hosea prescribes the only kind of treatment within his grasp, one based on rationality and creativity. He calls on his brethren to return to their belief in a rational God and to *their* creativity. Immediately after we hear about the child-sacrificing calf-kissers, we are told God's poetic assessment of His children:

> Therefore they shall be as the morning cloud, and as the early dew that passeth away, as the chaff that is driven with the whirlwind, . . . as the smoke out of the chimney. Yet I am the Lord, thy God from [since the time of] Egypt and thou shall know no god but me.

The artful Hosea draws on more metaphors to distinguish the smoke of irrational gods from the equally abstract but truthful laws of the Hebrew God, as Hosea's Chapter 13 moves deeper into poetry:

> I did know them in the wilderness, in the land of great draught. [Now, feeding in their new] pasture . . . they were filled [i.e., sated] ; therefore they have forgotten me. Therefore I will be as a lion: as a leopard by the way will I observe them: I will meet them as a bear that is bereaved of her whelps and will rend the caul of her heart, and there will I devour them as a lion: the wild beast shall tear them.

God's back-and-forth identification with a lion, then a bear, then a lion again, His self-portrait as a cruel beast and as an angry mother avenging her slaughtered "whelps," create a mirror image of the exulting child-murderers and the sexually-perverted calf-kissers. Hosea's verses, in which the mind of God and the minds of the whorish Jews chime together, reminds us that psychotherapy aims to re-harmonize the mind. And Hosea's poetry does seem intended as an artful therapy.

Hosea seems to have been among the first to realize that delusions of all kinds constitute a mental illness and not the handiwork of meddling gods. And he is also a gifted promoter of the idea that some artfully composed therapy might serve as a cure. When we speak of the art of medicine as a gift from Hippocrates and Galen, we might add the ancient Hebrews, too.

Why Hosea's chiming versification of wild bears and lions should work as therapy the prophet does not explain, but he does suggest that well-composed words might help the mind recompose itself. Hosea also fails to explain how the psychotherapist should proceed, but he ends his analysis with a description of a successful treatment, again in poetic language:

> I will be as the dew unto Israel: he shall grow as the lily . . . . His branches shall spread, and his branches shall spread as the olive tree, and the smell as Lebanon. They that dwell under his shadow shall return: they shall revive as the corn, and grow as the vine: the scent shall be as the wine of Lebanon. . . . Who is wise and shall understand these things, prudent and he shall know them? For the ways of the Lord are right, and the just shall walk in them: but the transgressors shall fall therein.

One need not believe that "the ways of the Lord are right" to accept the possibility that a skilled therapist might undertake a "prudent" search for the right words to treat delusional states of mind. Improvement in this realm, as Hosea suggests, might bring us closer to an ennobling polity, as lovely as the lily. Perhaps Hosea, with his prudent language, can be seen as an early advocate of "Talking Therapy," which was finally presented in a psychiatric setting three millennia later by Freud's colleague, Josef Breuer.

II: Isaiah Presents His Psychology of Idolatry

Hosea was not alone among the ancient Hebrew prophets to explore the psychological nature of idolatry, for the nation of Israel never freed itself from the delusional thinking of its neighbors and of its own people. Confronting idolatry thus became a national priority in the Israel of the Eighth century BCE, the time of Hosea in the Northern Kingdom of Ephraim, and of Isaiah in the Southern Kingdome of Judah.

Isaiah shared Hosea's conviction that delusional thinking was, for the Hebrews, a chronic mental illness treatable by the harmonizing power of poetry. In his poetic chapter 44, Isaiah begins with his major premise that there is only one Creator; then he moves on to his minor premise, that the Hebrews have abused their own God-given creativity even while retaining other valuable cognitive skills. If God is intelligent and creative, and man is created to be intelligent and creative, then it follows that mankind would do well to stick with their God-given creativity.

But the Hebrews often chose otherwise, ignoring Isaiah's poetry:

> Thus saith the Lord that made thee, and formed thee from the womb . . . . Fear not, O Jacob, my servant . . . . I am the first, and I am the last; and besides me there is no god; I know not any. They that make a graven image are all of them vanity: and delectable things shall not profit; and they

are their own witness; they see not, nor know that they may be ashamed. Who hath formed a god, or molten a graven image that is profitable for nothing? . . . The smith with the tongs both worketh in the coals, and fashioneth it with hammers. . . . The carpenter . . . heweth him down cedars . . . . he will take thereof, and warm himself; yea, he kindleth it and baketh bread; yea, he maketh a god and worshippeth it: he maketh it a graven image, and falleth down thereto . . . . and prayeth unto it, and saith, Deliver me; for thou art my god.

The proud, resourceful Hebrews, skillful in finding multiple uses for the same hewn log, render themselves ridiculous by adding a magical value to this log. Burning wood is a useful way to roast meat; but to idolaters, it is also ideal for the fabrication of gods.

Even worse, Isaiah insinuates that the Hebrews cannot even understand what Isaiah is telling them, as chapter 44 continues:

They have not known nor understood: for He hath shut their eyes, that they cannot see; and their hearts [i.e. mind], that they cannot understand. And none considereth in his heart neither is there knowledge nor understanding to say, I have burned part of it in the fire, yea, also I have baked bread upon the coals thereof; I have roasted flesh, and eaten it: and shall I make the residue thereof an abomination? Shall I fall down to the stock of a tree?

With perception dulled and understanding abolished, the troubled Israelites cannot see the folly of praying to the residuum of a log. Their God may have "shut their eyes," but He has also revealed that their understanding was so limited that they could not ask the crucial question for themselves: "Shall I fall down to the stock of a tree?" Presumably these besotted souls failed to perceive Isaiah's mockery.

But Isaiah offers a remedy. As his poetic chapter 44 continues, Isaiah bursts into a song that opens the possibility that the Hebrews might yet return to a harmonious and rational system of belief:

> O Israel, thou shalt not be forgotten of me. I have blotted out a thick cloud of thy transgressions, and, as a cloud thy sins: return unto me; for I have redeemed thee. Sing O ye heavens; for the Lord hath done it: shout ye, . . . break forth into singing, ye mountains, O forest, and every tree therein: for the Lord hath redeemed Jacob and glorified himself in Egypt.

Isaiah's prophecy presents idolatry as a slavish mental illness, from which the Hebrews in Egypt were rescued long ago, and from which the they might yet again be liberated by elevating themselves above "a thick cloud" of repetitive transgressions to sing the harmonious virtues of a monotheistic civilization.

CHAPTER FOUR
KING SAUL'S PSYCHOSIS

I: SAMUEL TESTS KING SAUL

Samuel, the first Judge of Israel, reminds Saul, early on in I Samuel, of his divinely ordained position as the King of Israel. And then Samuel immediately demands a treacherous test of the new King. Saul is to destroy the Amalekites, every one of them, including Agag their King, and every man and child, as well as all their herds. Saul performs so poorly in this test, that we can see that he suffers a mental disability.

In the background of this assignment to kill the Amalekites is the story that we have already encountered about Amalek. In Chapter 15, we will examine more thoroughly how the Tanach unifies its multiple references to this seemingly unimportant desert tribe, but here let us focus on this summary in Deuteronomy 15:17-19:

> Remember what Amalek did unto thee . . . when ye were come forth out of Egypt: How he met thee by the way, and smote the hindmost of thee, even all that were feeble behind thee, when thou wast faint and weary; and he [Amalek] had no awe of God. Therefore it shall be, when the Lord thy God hath given thee rest from all thine enemies . . . that thou shall blot out the remembrance of Amalek from under heaven; thou shalt not forget it.

As we have seen, this story not only features Amalek's brutal attack on the "faint" Hebrews fleeing from Egypt, but a complex cognitive task imposed on the former slaves. God commands that the Hebrews must not only "blot out the remembrance of Amalek" by exterminating them, but they must also "not forget" to remember them!

The ancient rabbis recognized that the Amalekites' hatred was motiveless, beyond reason, and therefore impor-tant, because it was representative of the antagonism that the Hebrew's anti-idolatrous way of rational living would inevitably provoke. They also knew that motiveless hatred was bestial. Cunning carnivores always attack the hindmost in a herd, the most sick and feeble.

Thus, the rabbis thought of the Amalekites as primitive creatures driven by hateful rage, against which an appro-priate cognitive defense was required. So, Deuteronomy 15 offers an example of that capacity: "Thou shalt blot out the remembrance of Amalek from under heaven; thou shall not forget it." Only human beings with well-developed cognitive abilities can remember and forget at the same time, thereby defending not only thirsty stragglers in the desert but also frail human life in general.

But the rabbis barely touched on the most important aspect of the Amalekites' hatred. Their contempt extended far beyond the few groaning slaves running from Egypt. They hated the Hebrews' God more than the Hebrews themselves: "and he [Amalek] had no awe of God." Because the Hebrews themselves often showed contempt for their God, as we shall see, they required a mental exercise to rehearse their obligation to obliterate their Amalekite tendencies.

But Saul cannot recall why he is attacking the Amalekites and King Agag, nor can he recall the marching orders that Samuel, Judge and Prophet, has given him. Though he does exterminate the Amalekites, he does not kill Agag, and he allows his soldiers to take the Amalekite herds as forbidden booty, thus undermining the goal of the expedition, which is to affirm an abstract idea and destroy its opposition, the idolatrous hatred of monotheism. Samuel is not pleased by Saul's failure to grasp his role, and the bungler can mount only a lame defense, showing that he lacks understanding of the meaning of his task, which is as bad as witchcraft, as we learn in I Samuel 15:17-23:

> And Samuel said to Saul, . . . the Lord sent thee on a journey, and said, Go and utterly destroy the sinners the Amalekites and fight against them until they be consumed. Wherefore then did thou not obey the voice of the Lord but did fly upon

the spoils, and did evil in the sight of the Lord? And Saul said unto Samuel, Yes I have obeyed the voice of the Lord, and have gone the way which the Lord sent me and have brought the King of Amalek, and have utterly destroyed the Amalekites. But the people took of the spoil, sheep and oxen, the chief of the things that should have been utterly destroyed, to sacrifice unto the Lord thy God in Gilgal. And Samuel said, Hath the Lord as great delight in burnt offerings and sacrifices as in obeying the voice of the Lord? . . . For rebellion is as the sin of witchcraft, and stubbornness is as iniquity and idolatry. . . . And Samuel said unto Saul, . . . the Lord has rejected thee from being king over Israel.

Saul asserts that he has done exactly what he has been asked to do, even while giving examples of his disobedience. Saul's self-contradictory mind thinks that believing anything he pleases is fine as long as he feels righteous about offering sacrifices to the Lord he obliviously offended. In contrast, Samuel asserts that irrational thinking is a form of "witchcraft," not fit for a king of a rational nation.

And that is only the beginning of the *Tanach*'s exploration of Saul's problematic psychology. Though Samuel has already told us "the Lord has rejected" Saul "from being King over Israel," his case history is so important that we must hear more of it. Saul has not only sinned against the Lord, but he has demonstrated that he lacks the cognitive skills to distinguish what he is doing from what he thinks he is doing. One might argue that Saul refrained from executing another king out of common decency, but that did not occur to Saul.

Rather, in Samuel I, 16:14-15, Saul provokes God to abandon him yet again:

> But the Spirit of the Lord departed from Saul, and an evil spirit from the Lord troubled him. And Saul's servants said unto him, Behold now, an evil spirit from God troubleth thee. Let our lord command . . . to seek out a man, who is a cunning player on the harp; and it shall come to pass when the evil spirit from God is upon thee, that he shall play with his hand, and thou shalt be well.

The King's servants come close to understanding Saul's troubles as a psychiatric disease, for they recommend a treatment that draws on the longstanding use of music to cure a troubled mind. If they had believed that Saul was suffering from a demon, they might have ordered an exorcist, but this was forbidden as "divination." So they asked the King to "to seek out a man who is a cunning player of a harp . . . and thou shalt be well." So, Saul complies:

> Provide me now a man that can play well, and bring him to me. Then answered one of the servants, . . . Behold, I have seen a son of Jesse the Bethlehemite that is cunning in playing, and a mighty valiant man, and a man of war, and prudent in matters, and a comely person, and the Lord is with him.

David's skills might have served him well in his treatment of Saul, if the diagnosis had been a mild depression, as many readers, ancient and modern, have believed. But depression is not the correct diagnosis.

Of course the narrator of Saul's story does not possess modern psychiatric knowledge, but he observes and records details that support Saul's correct diagnosis of a homicidal psychosis. During many centuries of psychological naivety, many commentators missed the diagnosis, but in about 1658 Rembrandt translated into pigment what he had read in his Bible, producing a probing portrait of *David Playing the Harp to Saul*:

Rembrandt positions David as a diminutive, child-like figure in the corner playing his harp, oblivious to the emotional upheaval of Saul. The royally-turbaned King uses the somber drape hanging to his left to wipe tears from his left eye as he rivets his sharp right eye on David, his imagined nemesis. Our astute artist, applying psychological insight, has Saul weeping for the kingship he is about to lose while he clings to a javelin with his right hand, preparing to hurl it at the boy musician. By portraying David as a cowering, harmless figure playing his harp, Rembrandt captures the King's paranoia about non-existent threats.

The perspicacious Rembrandt does not appear to see why this story was so important to the ancient Hebrews, but perhaps his very choice to paint this scene is itself an acknowledgment of the scene's Hebraic importance. Let us then examine Saul's story as a portrayal of a king who suffers psychosis in a society that values, or is supposed to value, rationality.

Soon after he is brought into Saul's court, David devises a way to defeat Goliath, without having to risk coming near the fierce warrior. He distracts the giant by taunting him about cutting off his head, to the point that the infuriated giant is blind to the possibility that a blathering youth without a sword could be dangerous. This gives cagey David the opening to arm his sling unnoticed. Quickly he fells the blowhard, and, without opposition, he cuts off the dead man's head, for the terrified Philistines have already fled.

The news of this triumph, as well as his further successes against the Philistines, earns David a fame that exacerbates Saul's psychological troubles. By the time David returns to Jerusalem with Goliath's head in hand, Saul has obliterated from his mind the very existence of supposedly dangerous David. Thus I Samuel 17:57-58:

And as David returned from the slaughter of the Philistine, Abner . . . brought him before Saul with the head of the Philistine in his hand. And Saul said to him, Whose son art thou, thou young man? And David answered, I am the son of thy servant Jesse the Bethlehemite.

Worse than this defensive amnesia, which is itself a sign of flight from reality, Saul is soon overtaken by paranoid jealousy when David wins more glory than the King in the ongoing Philistine war:

And . . . when David was returned form the slaughter of the Philistines, the woman came out of all cities of Israel, singing and dancing to meet King Saul with tabrets, with joy and with instruments of music. And the women answered one another as they played, and said, Saul has slain his thousands, and David his ten thousands. And Saul was very wroth . . . and he said what can he have more but the kingdom? And Saul eyed David from that day on [hence Rembrandt paints Saul's glowering right eye].

Saul's paranoid jealousy and his readiness to use the spear in his ever-ready right hand is intensified when women from all over Israel sang David's praises while mocking Saul's lesser accomplishments. The very music that was supposed to calm Saul inflames Saul's paranoia, as I Samuel continues:

And it came to pass on the morrow, that the evil spirit from God came upon Saul, as he sat in his house with his javelin his hand: and David played [the harp] with his hand, as at other times: and there was a javelin in Saul's hand. And Saul sought to smite David with the javelin; but he [David] slipped away out of Saul's presence, and he smote the javelin into the wall: and David fled and escaped that night.

That Saul madly throws his spear at shadows while trying to pin David to the wall demonstrates his unfitness to lead a rational nation.

And Saul's paranoia worsens. Based on an absurd story that supposedly proves Jonathan's perfidy, Saul condemns his loyal son to an undeserved death, just as he did in the case of David. During another battle with the Philistines, Jonathan is overwhelmingly triumphant, but he unknowingly failed to heed his father's command that his soldiers refuse all food on the day of battle.

For this minor offense, Saul wants his son executed. Though Jonathan mounts a rational defense, explaining that he never heard his father's prohibition, which was in any case counter-productive. Saul, pre-occupied by his paranoid need to "be avenged on my enemies," who include, in Saul's disturbed mind, not only David and the Philistines, but his own son. Saul is only barely restrained from filicide by his courtiers, as I Samuel 14 continues:

And the men of Israel were distressed that day: for Saul had abjured the people, saying, Cursed be the man that eateth any food until evening, that I may be avenged on my enemies. So none of the people tasted any food . . . . And when the people were come into the wood . . . behold, the honey dropped, but no man put his hand to his mouth: For the people feared the oath. But Jonathan heard not when his father charged the people: wherefore he put forth . . . his hand and dipped it in a honeycomb; and his eyes were enlightened [he saw how famished he was] . . . . Then said Jonathan [after learning that Saul had forbidden his soldiers to eat that day], My father has troubled the land: see, I pray you, how mine eyes have been enlightened, because I have tasted a little of this honey. How much more, if haply the peopled had eaten freely today . . . [would] there not been now a much greater slaughter among the Philistines?

Soon Saul learns that Jonathan complained about his father's tactical error, which was based on the bizarre belief that it was a good idea to make soldiers fast just when they most needed energy. Jonathan is likely correct when he claims that the battle would have been more successful had Saul not issued his foolish prohibition. Suffering minds often do project responsibility onto somebody else. In this way, Saul brands his son a traitor:

Then Saul said to Jonathan, Tell me what thou hast done. And Jonathan told him, and said, I did but tasted a little honey with the end of the rod that was in my hand, and, lo, I must die. And Saul answered, God do so and more also: for thou shall surely die.

Taking responsibility for one's own choices is not typical of those afflicted by psychosis. Thus Saul assigns the greater part of Jonathan's execution to God: Jonathan will "surely die," says Saul, and God will "do so and more."

This portrait of Saul's paranoid psychosis is often misrepresented as one of many Hebrew perversities that required a New Testament. But Saul's psychosis is not an example of Hebrew thinking, but a proxy for a thought disorder that ethical monotheism must confront and reject. Saul is not portrayed as a model to be admired, but as possessing a disqualifying mind. And indeed he was rejected.

Though Jonathan is rescued from Saul's madness, this is not the end of Saul's lengthy case history. In the end, Saul and his seven sons are killed in battle with the Philistines. Their bodies are sent back "into the land of the Philistines," where henchmen cut off Saul's head, and "they fastened his body to the wall of Beth-shan." This gruesome account of Saul's decapitation by the vengeful Philistines refers back to David's heroic decapitation of Goliath and Saul's paranoid attempt to fasten David's body to the wall with a spear.

By connecting David's decapitation of Goliath with Saul's own decapitation, the narrator of I Samuel asserts that violence is too often not in the service of good but in the service of irrationality. The Ancient Hebrews recognized that their island of monotheistic belief required defense against louts like Goliath, but they wanted to distinguish self-defense from irrational violence, which they loathed, especially if exhibited by their very first king, Saul, and by his replacement, too.

The story of David's decapitation of Goliath was not meant as a purely heroic act, for the celebrated King David also suffered from his own violent tendencies,and his libidinous excesses, too.

CHAPTER FIVE:
KING DAVID'S MANIC-DEPRESSIVE DISORDER

I: LESS A KING AND MORE OF EVERYTHING ELSE

Poet Laureate, a renowned harpist, a valiant man of arms, a ladies' man, a surreptitious murderer, and beloved by his people for 3,000 years, King David was submitted in the *Tanach* to a psychological scrutiny long before such a thing was known to exist. The sages of ancient Israel, as well as a long line of their rabbinic followers, noted David's sins, but these were discussed in a religious light, as sins usually are. But a deeper understanding of this complex man was actually provided in the *Tanach* itself, where a careful reader can find insights into this King's rich and troubled mind.

A man of great energy and talent, with a great lust for life, David could not control his wives, his sons, his army, or himself. The narrator of the two Books of Samuel composes the details of King David's life in a way that might lead a modern psychiatrist to diagnose this troubled King as suffering a bipolar-affective disorder, now called BAD.

Of course, it is more than problematic to make a medical diagnosis millennia after the supposed facts were recorded in a text that is often thought to be more imaginative than historical. But, as with any literary work focused on a hero's disturbing behavior, such as Shakespeare's *King Lear*, a psychological approach will serve well to unify David's troubled history.

Let us start with David's audacious decision to challenge Goliath, the champion of the Philistines, despite King Saul having warned the young lion against his foolish plan in I Samuel 17:

> Now the Philistines gathered their armies to battle . . . . And there went out a champion out of the camp of the Philistines, named Goliath of Gath, whose height was six cubits and a span . . . . And the staff of his spear was like a weaver's beam; and his spear's head weighed six hundred shekels of iron . . . . And the Philistine said, I defy the armies of Israel this day; give me a man that we may fight together. When Saul and all Israel heard those words of the Philistine, they were dismayed and greatly afraid. And all the men of Israel, when they saw the man, fled from him, and were sore afraid. . . . And David said to Saul, Let no man's heart fail because of him; thy servant will go and fight with the Philistine. And Saul said to David,

Thou art not able to go against this Philistine . . .
for thou art but a youth, and he a man of war from
his youth.

Even the psychologically handicapped Saul can grasp
that David, with no combat experience, is foolish in believing that he can overcome this battle-hardened giant. In
answering Saul, the future King employs the same idiomatic
language about a bear and a lion that Hosea used to express
the will of God, as we saw earlier. But in the fairy-tale-like
version that David tells, what is elevated is David's manic
self-assurance:

And David said unto Saul, thy servant kept his
father's sheep and there came a lion and a bear, and
took the lamb out of the flock: And I went out after
him [i.e., the bear] and smote him and delivered it
out of their [his] mouth: and when he arose against
me, I caught him [the bear] by the beard, and smote
him, and slew him. . . . . Thy servant slew both the
lion and the bear: and this Philistine [Goliath] shall
be one of them, seeing he hath defied the armies of
the living God.

Apparently thinking that his fairytale will persuade
Saul of his battle-readiness, David tells the King how he
rescued a lamb from both a bear and a lion by snatching
the lamb from the very maw of disaster. That he easily slew
these ferocious beasts, David reasons, is sufficient proof that
he can easily slay Goliath, whose height is a mere ten feet, a

cubit being approximately eighteen inches and a span about half that.

David is convinced that he can easily catch Goliath "by the beard" and slaughter him. His story draws on the creativity that he will later demonstrate in his psalms, but here it is nothing but hubris, if not mania. For even the experienced warriors in Saul's army have already fled from the terrifying giant.

The ancient rabbis ignored David's bravado, accepting his success as another example of God's protection of His chosen people, just as He did when He drowned the Egyptian charioteers as they pursued the Hebrews across a miraculously opened channel in the Red Sea. But the writer of the story of David and Goliath does not seem to be interested in miracles. He is more interested in showing David's manic zeal, his grandiosity (an actual psychiatric term).

Despite Saul's warning, David rushes to the frontlines to confront Goliath. Saul can do no more than equip the boy-soldier with sword and armor. But hyper-heroic David promptly discards these weighty items, having never been trained to use them:

> And David said to Saul, I cannot go with these; for I have not proved [tested] them. And David put them off him . . . . And it came to pass, when the Philistine . . . came and drew nigh to meet David, that David hasted, and ran toward the army to meet the Philistine. And David put his hand in his bag, and took thence a stone and slang it, and smote the

Philistine in the forehead, the stone sunk into his forehead; and he fell upon the earth . . . . So David prevailed upon the Philistine with a sling and with a stone; but there was no sword in the hand of David. Therefore David ran, and stood upon the Philistine, and took his[Goliath's] sword out of the sheath thereof . . . and cut off his head therewith.

This story in both Hebrew and the King-James translation races along at a galloping pace, which matches the rapid speech characteristic of maniacal patients. David runs hastily here and there, and then, in a single sentence packed with verbs, he puts his hand in his bag, takes out a stone, slings it, smites the Philistine in the forehead, the stone sinks into his forehead, and Goliath falls upon the earth. To contrast normal speech with this machinegun-like pace (a current psychiatric term for pressured, manic speech) the narrator slows the rhythm to a normal cadence as he ambles through a calm summary of what has just occurred:

So David prevailed upon the Philistine with a sling and with a stone; but there was no sword in the hand of David.

Then the rhythm picks up again, as David suddenly plunges into more action. Another verb-packed sentence captures the urgency of David's need to act, even when action is not necessary: He must decapitate the giant even though the giant is already dead and the Philistines are already panic-stricken:

Therefore, David ran, and stood upon the Philistine, and took his sword out of the sheath thereof
. . . and cut off his head therewith.

David's daring victory over Goliath made him a "mighty
valiant man," but his exuberant slaying of Goliath was only
the first display of his overdriven talents. Eventually he suffered the usual setbacks that befall those with manic drives.
We soon learn that David's mania turns out to be a funda-
mental defiance of the Hebrew God. For manic irrationality eventually fails, often leading to idolatry, as we shall see.

II: David's Cunning Succeeds for a Time

We soon see David at his clever best, before he blus-
tered into disaster. When Jonathan convinces his dear
friend that he must flee to save his life from Saul's paranoid
wrath, David of course knows what to do. But his flight
soon forces him into more dangers, for the paranoid Saul
still focuses his primitive cunning on David, having placed
spies everywhere, with orders to capture David for execution. One of these henchmen is Achish, the King of Gath,
Goliath's hometown.

When David arrives in the court of Achish, he quickly intuits that this King is Saul's agent, and thus a mortal danger; he must immediately craft an effective defense.
Sly David quickly turns himself into a drooling madman, figuring that this is just the trick to outsmart Achish
(Shakespeare borrows this trick when he has Hamlet say, "I

perchance hereafter shall think meet/ To put an antic dispo-sition on."). And indeed the suborned King of Gath thinks that the drooling maniac before him must be an impostor, certainly not the famous slayer of Goliath:

> And David . . . was sore afraid of Achish the King of Gath. And he changed his behavior . . . and feigned himself mad in their hands [the hands of Achish's servants], and scrabbled on the doors of the gate, and let his spittle fall down upon his beard. Then said Achish unto his servants, Lo ye see the man is mad, wherefore then have ye brought him to me?

David's quick thinking is clearly superior to Saul's par-anoid plotting. For only a leader who is cognitively skill-ful can lead a people devoted to a rational and just God. But cleverness alone is not sufficient. The ancient rabbis believed that David's sins disqualified him from building the First Temple, which was left to Solomon, the son born to him by Bathsheba.

III THE BRILLIANT KING WAVERS

But God allowed David to blunder on, like Cain, so that he and his descendants could refocus their pumped-up drives on nobler goals.

The narrator of the Book of Samuel, no hagiographer, presents David as a righteous monotheist only in the sense that he was a work in progress, hobbled by his psychological

flaws. Consider the events concerning David's moving Israel's Capital from Hebron to Jerusalem. The story, told in II
Samuel 6, features two puzzling events, both of which are
linked to David's problematic capacities to lead Israel.

The first of these events involves Uzzah's fatal misstep
on the road to Jerusalem. He reached out to steady the ark of
the Lord, which was being shaken off the cart by the labor-
ing oxen. God immediately kills Uzzah for his supposed
error, a shockingly severe punishment for a well-intended
act that has puzzled commentators since antiquity. How
else should Uzzah, whose name means "strength," prevent
brute animals from desecrating the ark of the Lord?

> And when they came to Nachson's threshing
> floor, Uzzah put out his hand to the ark of God,
> and took hold of it; for the oxen shook it. And the
> anger of the Lord was kindled against Uzzah; and
> God smote him there; and there he died by the ark
> of God. And David was displeased . . . And David
> was afraid of the Lord that day, and he said, How
> shall the ark of the Lord come to me?

Though Uzzah is the one who dies, the focus of the story is on David, who sees the demise of Uzzah as a divine
remonstrance aimed at him. Immediately after Uzzah is
struck down, we learn that "David was afraid of the Lord
that day," so worried that he blurts out, "How shall the ark
of the lord come to me?" David then promptly carries "the
ark of God" to the nearby home of Obed-edom, apparently

fearing that Obed-edom was more "blessed by the Lord" than he himself. Thus David defers to a man whose name means "Servant-of-Edom," an idolatrous people on the border of Israel:

> So David would not remove the ark of the Lord unto him into the city of David: but David carried it aside into the house of Obed-edom the Gittite. . . . And the Lord blessed Obed-edom and all his household.

The rabbis struggled to explain the harshness of Uzzah's punishment and its meaning to David. Unable to arrive at a convincing interpretation, they faulted Uzzah for violating Numbers 4:15, which forbids the touching of sacred instruments when they were being moved within the Temple. Supposedly, Uzzah desecrated God's realm by trying to safeguard the Torah! But the details of the story itself focuses our attention elsewhere, not on Uzzah's sin but on David's identification with Uzzah. David reveals himself by identifying with a punished man who reached too far.

This reading, suggested by the literary skill of Samuel's author, is concordant with the second story connected to the transport of the ark to Jerusalem. When he finally arrives with the ark of the Lord in Jerusalem, David again reveals himself as one who extends himself too far, this time lewdly. His wife, Michal, the daughter of King Saul, is there to observe the royal travesty:

And as the ark of the Lord came into the city of David, Michal Saul's daughter looked through a window, and saw king David leaping and dancing before the Lord; and she despised him in her heart. . . . And Michal came out to meet David, and said, How glorious was the king of Israel today, who uncovered himself today in the eyes of the handmaids of his servants, as one of the vain fellows shamelessly uncovers himself. And David said unto Michal, It was before the Lord, which chose me before thy father, and before all his house, to appoint me ruler over the people of the Lord, over Israel: therefore will I play before the Lord. And I will be more vile than thus, and will be base in mine own sight: and of the maidservants which thou hast spoken of, of them shall I be held in honor. Therefore Michal the daughter of Saul had no child unto the day of her death.

In this passage, composed with literary craft, we easily catch Michal's sarcastic tone as she congratulates her husband about "how glorious" he was in exposing himself to "the handmaids of his servants." Also well-captured is David's tone-deaf bragging about how much he will enjoy the "honor" bestowed on him by the very handmaids before whom he has lewdly danced. David forgets that these lowly handmaids, servants of servants, are particularly unworthy his attention, or maybe he does remember. His intention, he tells Michal, is to "be more vile . . . and will be base in my own sight."

Despite David's vulgarity, rabbis have almost universally blamed Michal for mocking her husband, and they believed that God later punished her with infertility because of her confrontational behavior. But the context suggests otherwise: The philandering David probably abandoned the wife who criticized his licentious mania. In this view, Michal was not punished but ignored, not infertile but banished form the marital bed for correctly recognizing her husband's manic self-display. It was David himself who was punished, not by infertility precisely, but by the death of a child he fathered with Bathsheba. David was vulgar; Michal was shamed.

And David's sexual impropriety gets worse. The famous story of his murderous libido provoked by the irresistible beauty of Bathsheba begins when David was busy managing from afar his war with the idolatrous Ammonites under the command of General Joab. Suddenly David's interest shifts from warfare to the pursuit of an infatuation, as if he were illustrating Freud's characterization of the primitive drives of libido and aggression being interchangeable, as they were in Homer's *Iliad*, where the beauty of Helen launched a thousand ships. A similarly sordid tale appears in II Samuel 11:

> And it came to pass in the evening, that David arose off his bed, and walked upon the roof of the king's house: and from the roof he saw a woman washing herself: and the woman was very beautiful to look upon. And David sent and enquired after the woman. And one said, Is not this Bathsheba

. . . , the wife of Uriah the Hittite? And David sent a messenger and took her uncleanness: and she returned unto her house. And the woman conceived, and sent and told David, and said, I am with child. And David sent to Joab, saying, Send me Uriah the Hittite. . . . And when Uriah was come unto him, David demanded of him how Joab did, and how the people did, and how the war prospered.

Just as in the story of his triumph over Goliath, the story of David's seduction of Bathsheba moves at maniacal speed. In a flash, David glimpses Bathsheba, beds her, impregnates her, and sets in motion his plan to kill her husband. Clearly, the galloping rhythm of this story and its impious details (the good King takes the gorgeous lady during the "uncleanness" of her period, which is strictly forbidden by Mosaic Law, precisely because the sanctity of procreation must be carefully distinguished from bloodlust). Righteous readers of the *Tanach* understand this abstractly, but in 1654 Rembrandt portrayed the alluring power of Bathsheba's fondling of David's enticing letter:

Rembrandt knows how to use paint to catch the conscience of the King, so that the viewer has no trouble seeing why this redhead, commands not only the lust of this King, but his aggressive drives, too.

A clever schemer, David supposedly brings Uriah to his court to learn about the war's progress, but this is a ruse to disguise his true motive, which is to have Uriah carry his own death sentence back to General Joab.

As David plots Uriah's death, Uriah unknowingly instructs his King about the proper mental equipment and values of a true leader of Israel; but this has no effect on the King's libidinous machinations:

> And David said to Uriah, Go down to thy house, and wash thy feet . . . . But Uriah slept at the door of the king's house with all the servants . . . . And when they had told David, saying Uriah went not down to his house, David said unto

> Uriah, . . . why then did thou not go down unto thy
> house? And Uriah said unto David, The ark, and
> Israel and Judah, abide in tents; and my lord Joab,
> and the servants of my lord, are encamped in the
> open fields; shall I then go into my house, to eat and
> to drink and to lie with my wife? as thou livest and
> thy soul liveth, I will not do this thing. . . . And
> it came to pass in the morning that David wrote a
> letter to Joab, and sent it by the hand of Uriah . . .
> saying, Set thee Uriah in the forefront of the hot-
> test battle, and retire ye from him, that he may be
> smitten and die.

We cannot miss David's duplicity, his cruel sending a letter to Joab placed in Uriah's own hand, commanding the noble messenger's death (this vile trick was also borrowed by Shakespeare in *Hamlet*, where the noble Prince has Rosencrantz and Guildenstern carry their own death sentences to the King of England), nor can we miss David's deafness to Uriah's modeling of a more kingly mind.

We might, then, go deeper into the psychological investigation of David's behavior. Like many patients who suffer from manic episodes, David suffered from depression. Thus, the *Tanach* comes close to demonstrating that this celebrated King suffered from what we now call a bipolar-affective disorder, a diagnosis certainly not available in ancient Israel, and not available in the West for another 3,000 years.

From the details recorded in the Book of Samuel, we learn that David suffered the jumbled symptoms of both mourning and melancholia. "Mourning and Melancholia" is the title of an essay by Freud, who distinguished the one from the other. Mourning comes on rapidly and is comparatively brief, usually provoked by a shocking loss of a loved one. Melancholia, the ancient malady we now call depression, usually comes on slowly, dominates the mind more broadly, and, having taken command of the brain's chemistry, can last much longer, even permanently, impairing sleep, cognition, appetite, ability to find pleasure or interest in anything.

Robert Burton's *The Anatomy of Melancholy*, published in 1621, ten years after the publication of the King-James Bible, was likely influenced by the original Hebrew portrayal of David's bipolar-affective disorder, as well as by Reverend Burton's own experience with depression and his wide reading and careful observation. How the writer of the Book of Samuel came to know so much about the symptomology of melancholia is a mystery, but perhaps he knew because he observed.

Here is the story of how David came to mourn the death of his son born to Bathsheba. David's mourning was not provoked by a shock to his limbic system, nor was it true mourning. It stemmed again from his over-driven guile, brought into daylight by Nathan the prophet, as told in II Samuel 12. Nathan chooses a parable to focus David's attention on the fact that he has committed a mortal sin. The parable is a tear-jerker, easy for most people with David's cognitive skills to interpret, concerning a rich man, the owner of "exceeding many flocks and herds," who for his own pleasure, steals from a poor man his single, beloved "ewe lamb, . . . it did eat of his own meat, and drank of his own cup, and lay in his bosom, and was unto him as a daughter."

But David does not easily interpret the parable. His lust for Bathsheba has blunted his capacity to interpret metaphoric language. He takes the story literally, unable to see that the rich man's theft of a ewe lamb is a version of his expropriation of Bathsheba. Dumbly, he vilifies the rich man and wants him executed, as if he were an actual man. Here Nathan has to interpret for David, whose impulsive anger has overcome his intelligence. Though he wises-up, he soon thereafter engages in more chicanery:

> And Nathan said to David, Thou art that man. Thus saith the Lord God of Israel . . . . Wherefore hast thou despised the commandment of the Lord, to do evil in his sight? thou hast killed Uriah . . . . and hast taken his wife to be thy wife . . . . because of this deed, thou has given great occasion to the enemies of the Lord to blaspheme, the child that is born to unto thee shall surely die. .
> . . And it came to pass on the seventh day, that the child died . . . . And the servants of David feared to tell him that the child was dead: for they said, Behold, while the child was yet alive, we spake unto him he would not hearken unto our voice: how will he then vex himself, if we tell him the child is dead. But when David saw that his servants whispered, David perceived the child was dead. . . . Then David arose from the earth, and washed, and anointed himself, and changed his apparel . . . and

when he required, they set bread before him, and he did eat. Then said the servants unto him, What thing is this that thou hast done? Thou didst fast and weep for the child, while it was alive; but when the child was dead, thou didst rise and eat bread. And he said, While the child was yet alive, I fasted and wept: for I said, Who can tell whether God will be gracious to me, that the child may live? But now he is dead, can I bring him back again? I shall go to him, but he shall not return to me.

The narrator here crafts the story of the child's sickness and death so that David *appears* to suffer from a bizarre mixture of symptoms signifying both mourning and melancholia, but typical of neither. This jumbled symptomology seems false, and that is because it is created to sound false. When the child was very sick but still living, David withdrew from the world, deaf to his servants, and refused to eat, as is often true of those mourning.

But this is not typical of a father worrying about his sick child; an actual father in this situation is anxiously attentive, eager to hear details of every development. And when the beloved child dies, the bereaved parent usually falls into mourning, which slowly improves. Because David seemed depressed when his child was sick, and full of energy after the child died, the narrator, quite impressively, appears to know enough psychology to interrogate David's peculiar behavior.

So he has David explain what he was thinking. The crafty King fasted and wept when the child was still alive not because he was worried or depressed, but because he was trying to manipulate God into granting him a favorable outcome ("Who can tell whether God will be gracious to me, that the child may live?").

After the child dies, again drawing on his self-serving skills, David, gets up, washes, anoints himself in his kingly garments, and eats, because there was no point to doing anything else. He finishes the rationalization of his behavior by turning his attention to his preserved power to act: "I shall go to him, but he shall not return to me." This could be read as mournful realization that he, the King, will eventually suffer the same fate as the child, but this interpretation denies the self-aggrandizement of the slayer of Goliath. What David seems to have in mind is a selfish acceptance of cold reality, "There's nothing to be done now for the child; death is inevitable for all, so I will get up and live."

But the whirligig of life does not last forever. And we soon learn that just as David enacted a madman to outsmart Achish and then demonstrated actual madness, he now developed true depression after mimicking signs of both mourning and melancholia.

David's melancholia emerges after a long, bitter entanglement in the incestuous rivalries and fratricide of his several sons, which results in the murder of his beloved son, Absalom, for whose death David was partly responsible. By the time of his death, Absalom had helped himself to the royal concubines, and planned to proclaim himself King of Israel in Hebron, as we are told in II Samuel 15:10-16:21:

> Absalom sent spies throughout all the tribes of Israel, saying, As soon as ye hear the sound of the trumpet, then ye shall say, Absalom reigneth in Hebron. And Achitophel said unto Absalom, Go unto the father's concubines. . . . And all Israel shall hear that thou art abhorred by thy father . . . . So they spread Absalom a tent upon the house; and Absalom went in unto his father's concubines in the sight of all Israel.

David here suffers the poetic justice of having imposed on him the same kind of intrigue that enabled him to have his way in war and love.

This kind of behavior is of course not appropriate for any King of Israel, be he David or Absalom.

After Absalom continues his rebellious activities, David sends his most loyal soldiers to quash the insurrection, which is accomplished. When David learns of his army's victory in II Samuel 18-19, he expresses the hope that Absalom is still safe, for he still loves his rebellious son. After the first, nervous messenger from the battlefield self-protectively avoids David's questions by claiming to be ignorant, David corners a second officer, Cushi, to learn the fate of his beloved son. Cushi carefully frames his account of Absalom's violent death. His words and his tone capture the nature of the touchy situation he is in; and David's response to the implicit bad news captures *his* true feelings:

And Cushi answered, The enemies of my lord the king, and all that rise against thee to do thee hurt [should] be as that man is. And the king was much moved and went up to the chamber over the gate and wept: and as he went thus he said, O my son Absalom, my son, my son Absalom! would God I had died for thee, O Absalom, my son, my son! . . . . And the people gat them by stealth into the city, as people being ashamed steal away when they flee in battle. But the king covered his face, and the king cried with a loud voice, O my son Absalom, O Absalom, my son, my son!

Cushi's strategic answer to David's question starts with a prayerful wish for the King's well-being, a blessing meant to soften the bad news, which is actually rolled into the blessing. This strategy helps little to assuage David's expected response, which the narrator carefully crafts to indicate that David is now truly in mourning. David's constant weeping, his iteration of "my son, my son," and his wish that he could have died in place of his son—these lamentations do indeed resemble true mourning. His feelings are so intense that witnesses must flee the pitiable spectacle. Unlike his manipulative performance while his young child was dying, David now falls into genuine mourning, and this soon develops into an endless melancholy that persists until he recovers at the very end of his life.

Like Cain, David lived long enough to turn his creativity away from cunning into poetry, his libido from lust to a love of his righteous God, his aggression into an energetic devotion of the Almighty.

In this view, it is perhaps not surprising that the narrator weaves into his story of David's evolving psychology an allusion to Cain and Able. This occurs as part of a ruse concocted by Joab to get David, the master of ruses, to forgive Absalom before matters deteriorate further.

Joab sends an anonymous "handmaid" to convince David to pardon her fictitious son for having killed his brother, as told in II Samuel 14:6-7:

> And thy handmaiden had two sons, and they strove together in the field, and there was none to part them, but the one smote the other, and slew him. And, behold, the whole family is risen against thine handmaid, and they said, Deliver him that smote his brother, that we may kill him ... and his heir also ... and they shall not leave to my husband neither name nor remainder upon the earth.

Unlike his failure to recognize himself quickly in Nathan's parable, on this occasion David can at least guess that Joab must have arranged the handmaid's visit. But the troubled King cannot guess Joab's purpose, nor can he recognize that the seemingly forthright handmaid is there to manipulate him by praising his wisdom and thereby sweet-talk him into forgiving Absalom. While playing on David's attraction to handmaids, she can count on the fact that David, hampered by his melancholia, will not recall that the *Tanach* forbids brute revenge or punishing a child for the sins of his father (See Deuteronomy 24:16 and Ezekial 18:20). But this savvy handmaid does count on David recognizing that her son, the Cain figure, deserves to be protected, just like murderous Cain, who committed exactly the same crime. And this savvy handmaid must have learned from Joab that the best way to accomplish her goal was first to admit that Joab composed her spiel and then play on David's need to please handmaids, especially one as forthcoming as she. Here is the sly lady's smooth approach to her King:

> . . . thy servant Joab . . . put all these words in the mouth of thine handmaid . . . and my lord is wise, according to the wisdom of an angel of God, to know all things that are in the earth.

Though the handmaid does accomplish the goal of persuading the flattered King to grant a reprieve for her imaginary son, this is not her real purpose. King David grants the requested reprieve, unaware that he has been led to forgive a fictitious person so that the handmaid might more easily maneuver the King into forgiving Absalom.

This surprisingly complicated story tells us much about the Ancient Hebrews' understanding of the psychology of persuasion and manipulation. Why is this important? One must develop a savvy rationality in order to submit to the wisdom of ethical monotheism and thereby avoid the snares of cunning manipulation. At this point in his long career,

David still finds it difficult to accept his God's often-puzzling demands for ethical behavior. With a mind easily manipulated by the likes of Joab and his handmaid, he cannot serve well as a King of Israel.

David, from beginning to end, illustrates both all that is necessary to be King of Hebrew wisdom, and all the pitfalls on the road to that eminence. A Hebrew King must be intelligent but not wily, dedicated but not maniacally so, a master of a harmonized mind, capable of playing the lyre, but free from the cacophony of psychopathology.

IV: David's Therapeutic Transformation

By the end of his story, David undergoes a transformation that overcomes his manic-depressive tendencies and helps him marshal his creative skills and thereby achieve a therapeutic resolution. In his poetry, which begins at the end of II Samuel and continues into his Psalms, David rises from a maniacally valiant man to a more harmonious and rational being.

David's artful transformation may be a poor substitute for our modern, pharmacologic treatment of BAD. But perhaps the ancient Hebrews have something to add to modern psychiatry, a field in which there is still much to be learned about mood disorders.

In II Samuel 22, the narrator allows David to speak for himself in language that resembles the musical tone of his famous Psalms:

And David spake unto the Lord the words of this song in the day that the Lord had delivered him out of the hand of all his enemies, and out of the hand of Saul . . . . When the waves of death compassed me, the floods of ungodly men made me afraid; the sorrows of hell compassed me about; the snares of death prevented [confronted] me. In my distress I called upon the Lord, and cried to my God; and he did hear my voice . . . . He made darkness pavilions round about him, dark waters, and thick clouds in the skies . . . . Through the brightness before him were coals of fire kindled.

A pious devotion to the Hebrew God was and is the essential standard demanded of both ancient and modern Hebrews, but to achieve true piety, and thus avoid the pseu-do-piety of his dancing lewdly with the Torah, David must first master his mind. The narrator of the Book of Samuel focuses our attention on poetry as an artful therapeutic by placing it in his conclusion of David's history.

The idea that poetry itself might have therapeutic effects is not unknown in the literature of modern psychotherapeu-tics, but it is difficult to take David's ancient poetry as mak-ing any serious contribution to the treatment of manic-de-pressive disease. But there it is for our consideration.

In the extensive case history of David, we learn that this beloved King of Israel achieved piety belatedly. Eventually, he saw that he had been separating himself from his God, to the point that God has withdrawn from the rebellious King: "He made darkness pavilions round about Him, dark waters, and thick clouds in the skies." These words are such an astute observation of depression that they recall William Styron's description of his own depression in *Darkness Visible*.

By the time we arrive to Psalm 35, David is moving from a manic-depressive state to a more composed and joyful piety. Despite the many accolades this most admired King acquired over the millennia, he did not show much piety until the end.

> Plead my cause, O Lord, with them that strive with me: fight against them that fight against me . . . . But in my adversity they rejoiced, and gathered themselves together: yea, the abjects [lowlifes] gathered themselves against me, and I knew it not; they did tear me, and ceased not: With hypocritical mockers in feasts, they gnashed upon me with their teeth . . .. Let them be ashamed and brought to confusion together they who rejoice at my hurt . . . . . Let them shout for joy, and be glad, that favor my righteous cause: yea, let them say continually, Let the Lord be magnified, which hath pleasure in the prosperity of his servant.

Early in this poem, David is overwhelmed and paranoid, claiming that his enemies gathered against him even though he "knew it not." By the end, David manages to project confusion back onto those lowlifes who mock him at cannibalistic feasts by gnashing upon him "with their teeth." This bombastic language offloads David's hyperbolic violence expressed in his beheading of Goliath and in other military adventures, thus freeing him to embrace a joyful piety.

Even if this successful transformation of David cannot be taken seriously as a substitute for science-based psychotherapy, and even if the modern reader is not a bit interested in piety or poetry, David's psychiatric history presents valuable, durable truths.

A pious reverence for ethical law arises only in a healthy, creative mind. Irrational thinking underlies idolatry and other forms of mad behavior. Even intelligent and creative minds can be undermined by chaotic psychopathology, and for those souls who fall into difficulties like those of the crafty, valiant, creative, adulterous, murderous, and manic-depressive King David, a particularly well-woven therapy might be crafted.

Just as David spoke to his Lord at the end of his life in poetry, so too did Moses. Soon to die, Moses addressed his wandering people in a song, recorded in Deuteronomy 32, just as they were about to enter the Land of Israel without him.

> And Moses spake in the ears of all the congregation of Israel the words of this song, . . . Give ear, O ye heavens, and I will speak; and hear O earth, the words of my mouth, my doctrine [understanding] shall drop as the rain, my speech shall distill as the dew, as the small rain upon the tender herb, and as the showers upon the grass.

These words are inscribed in the Torah in a format designed especially for poetry, not by divisions into stanzas, but by phrases separated by longish, empty spaces, as is the case in the passage cited just above, and in the passage cited from II Samuel 22. The rendition of Moses' and David's last words as poetry, described by both Moses and David as "song," highlights the creative and thoughtful nature of the Hebraic perspective.

David's Psalms emphasize the rhythms of creativity, the mind's search for harmony. This kind of understanding, the Hebrews believed, is necessary to distinguish the commands of a righteous God from the jarring, literal-minded thinking of idolaters. So the repentant King David sings, preparing the way for chanting in great Cathedrals and small synagogues and churches around the world. Even those who believe in no God might recognize that a harmonious mind is not only a comfort in itself but the only possible sanctuary for the idea of a just society.

Here, in Psalm 33, is David's evolved view of this subject:

Rejoice in the Lord, O ye righteous [Hebrew *Tsadikim*, the just]: for praise is comely for the upright. Praise the Lord with harp: sing unto him with the psaltery and an instrument with ten strings. Sing unto him a new song; play skillfully with a loud noise [a moving call from a ram's horn]. For the word of the Lord is right; and all his works are done in truth.

The mind is like a musical instrument. When its beliefs harmonize with a rational system of thought, the mind of a righteous soul might indeed find a satisfactory "truth"; without this harmony, even the intelligent King David could not stumble on any reliable system of truth or justice, no matter how well he played the harp.

CHAPTER SIX
Samson's Defective Executive Function

I: The Executive Brain

In 2001, Dr, Elkhonon Goldberg, a student of Alexander Luria, Russia's most esteemed neuropsychologist, published *The Executive Brain: Frontal Lobes and the Civilized Mind*, and since then the concept of executive function has penetrated further and further into the practice of both psychiatry and neurology.

We find, for instance, that executive function deteriorates early in the course of Alzheimer's disease. Patients become particularly inept when necessity forces them to weave from a complicated stream of stimuli the best possible response to a difficult and urgent problem. Living in a complex, civilized world, with its ever-changing ideas, rules, and demands, requires constant adjustment to rapidly varying stimuli.

Say Grandma is traveling with her daughter and granddaughter to a new city, a trip like many others that this three-generation family has enjoyed in the past. But Grandma now repeats herself every once in a while without realizing that she had just asked the same question. This has not bothered her or her family. In the setting of having her own small apartment in her daughter's home, she has been living semi-independently, driving her own car to the same locations nearby, never getting lost. She was also taking short walks from home, always choosing the same routes with no problems finding her way home. Every night, after enjoying a prepared meal with her family, she reads in bed, but she recently switched from books to magazines, having found that by the time she would get to chapter three in her book she couldn't recall what occurred in chapter one.

After checking into the hotel that was chosen by her daughter, Grandma goes for a walk alone in the new city, having forgotten to ask for a map from the receptionist. She quickly loses her way, unable to recall the name of her hotel or the name of the street it was on. Her failing memory caused her present difficulty, but Grandma is now facing a more difficult challenge than remembering the name of her hotel. In her anxious state, she must quickly devise a plan, taking into consideration all the stimuli bombarding her as well as the relevant possibilities and obstacles. She wishes that she had asked her granddaughter to accompany her on this suddenly confusing walk; she knows that the 10-year-old would be good at solving her problem.

Dr. Goldberg reminds us that the human frontal lobes are not only much larger than the frontal lobes of other primates, they are also more inter-connected with all other parts of the human brain. In a healthy state the capacious frontal lobes can draw on its many connections to render a plan that would likely meet all the demands of Grandma's current situation.

For example, a cognitively intact traveler would easily think to herself, "I'm confused probably because I'm sleep-deprived in a new place, but I can stop a passerby and explain that I have wandered about three quarters of a mile from my hotel. I can't recall its name or the name of its street, but it has four marble pillars surrounding the front door and it's across the street from a small park with a pond." If that didn't help she might ask directions from one of the passing cab drivers, knowing that they are familiar with their city's hotels.

However, Grandma's frontal lobes no longer have at their disposal enough useful connections. So she sits down on the curb and cries until a worried pedestrian has her taken to a nearby hospital.

Grandma's daughter must also deal with an unexpected difficulty. Fearing that her mother has suffered a bad accident, she calls nearby hospitals; this plan, the product of an intact executive function, allows the daughter to rescue her mother while keeping track of her own daughter's safety.

II. An Early Sign of Dementia

During thirty-five years of practicing neurology, I have heard many stories like that of Grandma, only to find that patients like Grandma can still perform fairly well on simple cognitive tests. One of these tests is the Mini-Cognitive Test, which evaluates the ability to recall three objects after being told to remember them for 5 minutes, and then to draw a clock accurately and set it to a specified time, say 11:20. As difficult as this may be, it is far less complicated then managing Grandma's new problem, which is why a failing executive function is often an early sign of Alzheimer's disease.

Thus, if a clinician uses evidence of declining executive function to diagnose Alzheimer's disease, appropriate treatment, aimed at slowing the disease's progression, can start at an earlier, more beneficial time.

Because evaluation of executive function is a recent addition to the practice of psychiatry and neurology, it is surprising to find that it has been studied by Shakespeare, especially in *Julius Caesar*, *Coriolanus*, and *Antony and Cleopatra*, and even earlier, in the ancient Hebrew Bible. Caesar, Coriolanus, and Antony all fail to recognize and act on the crucial details of their life-threatening situations, and so does the supposedly mighty Samson.

III: A Father and Son with Poor Executive Function

The usual interest in the fatal romance between Samson and Delilah focuses on either the titillating sex and the suicidal violence, or on the story's religious significance, but let us focus on the many details that reveal the problematic psychology of our hero. He makes poor choices and misuses his physical strength. Worst of all, he destroys a multitude of Philistines and himself without doing anything to end the Hebrews' longstanding war with these idolaters.

Samson, a wily military strategist and clever riddle maker, is not stupid, but with poor executive function he often acts before he puts together all the relevant details of the situations he is in. In colloquial English, we might say that Samson leaps before he thinks, goes off half-cocked, shoots off his mouth when he should remain silent, makes a mess of himself. The Philistines cut out his eyes easily only because he was already blind to obvious dangers. He was able to kill a lion bare-handedly, and he astutely picked up an ass's jawbone just when he needed a weapon to kill a regiment of Philistines, but he then fails to create a successful strategy to outwit his Philistine tormenters.

Instead, he ends his life by carrying out a foolish plan. He couldn't even keep in mind that he was a *nazir*, appointed by God to be a rational leader of a pious community. A modern neurologist or psychiatrist, who may not be interested in piety, would easily note Samson's pathologic executive function.

A careful clinical history of Samson might best start with the story of his father. Manoah is perhaps the stupidest man in the Bible. It just so happens that Dr. Goldberg distinguishes stupidity from low intelligence and smartness from high intelligence. An adult with a fully-developed executive function is smart, perhaps not among the gifted, but reliably able to solve complicated, real-life problems; his opposite is stupid, unable to make sense of complicated social situations. An author with a high score on an intelligence test might write award-winning fiction but lose a suitcase full of irreplaceable manuscripts in a French train station, as did Ernest Hemmingway, who was likely only temporarily confused, perhaps by depression (he eventually committed suicide). Dr. Elkhonon Goldberg would likely call Hemingway intelligent but with an impaired executive function that occasionally led him to stupid acts.

The author of the Book of Judges prepares his readers to note the endowment that inadequate Manoah bequeathed to his son. In this literary story, the writer presents Manoah's deficits as a prelude to Samson's similar inadequacies. This family resemblance, however, is certainly not an example of the heritability of human traits, a subject that would not be broached until the time of Mendel and Darwin.

Because Samson was chosen to be a Judge of a supposedly rational people, our narrator is particularly interested in demonstrating a distinction between the rationality required of the Hebrews and the irrationality of their idolatrous neighbors, especially the Philistines. That both Samson and King Saul died ensnared on the very turf of the idolatrous Philistines signals the Hebrew tendency to slip back into irrationality. Even today, the extinct Philistines remain an emblem of cultural vapidity.

In Judges 13:1-7, we are told how Manoah learned that his barren wife would bare him a son. Apparently Manoah is too stupid to be given the news firsthand, so the angel of the Lord communicates directly with Manoah's wise wife, here and later on:

> And the children of Israel did evil again in the sight of the Lord; and the Lord delivered them into the Philistines forty years. And there was a certain man of Zorah . . . whose name was Manoah; and his wife was barren, and bare not. And the angel of the Lord appeared unto the woman, and said unto her, Behold now, thou art barren and bearest not; but thou shall conceive, and bear a son . . . . Then the woman came and told her husband, saying, A man of God came unto me, and his countenance was like the countenance an angel of God, very terrible: but I asked him not whence he was, neither told he me his name: But he said unto me, Behold, thou shalt conceive, and bear a son; and now drink no wine nor strong drink, nor eat any unclean thing: for the child shall be a Nazerite to God from the womb to the day of his death.

Manoah's wife immediately recognizes that she is speaking with a man of God, and from his countenance, which was "very terrible," she can read that he is "an angel of the Lord." She does not ask this angel from whence he came, because she is wise enough to know the answer. Nor does she expect to be told his name, because the fact that he hasn't given her his name is sufficient to let her know that he is not a human wayfarer who would reliably introduce himself. And she easily recognizes that the diet prescribed to her by the angel of the Lord is not meant as sound nutritional advice but as a symbolic preparation for her son's sanctified mission. Samson is to be a Nazerite (*nazir* in Hebrew, a term that was later applied to Jesus), appointed to represent the sanctity of monotheism, which is an abstract concept not usually available to literalists, who prefer idolatry.

In contrast to his wife, Manoah is unable to read the abstract meaning of a symbolic diet; instead, he focuses on the need to offer literal food to a flesh-and-blood man of God; he cannot recognize that this man of God with a spiritual message does not eat. So slow Manoah offers to prepare dinner, thus revealing his inability to understand abstract thinking or metaphoric language. Only well-connected frontal lobes can marshal these capacities; neither crocodiles nor the Egyptians who worshiped them possess these capabilities, and neither did the many other idolaters from whom the ancient Hebrews wished to distinguish themselves.

Not himself a leader, Manoah trots "after" his wife as they go in search of the man of God. Thoughtless Manoah lacks sufficient executive function to behave appropriately when his wife, who easily remembers the way, brings him to the messenger:

> And Manoah arose and went after his wife, and came to the man, and said unto him, Art thou the man that spakest unto the woman? And he said, I am. [Then] Manoah asks, . . . How shall we order the child, and how shall we do unto him? And the angel of the Lord said unto Manoah . . . . She may not eat anything that cometh of the vine, neither let her drink wine of strong drink, nor eat any unclean thing: all that I have commanded her let her observe. And Manoah said unto the angel of the Lord, I pray thee, let us detain thee until we shall have made ready a kid for thee. And the angel of the Lord said unto Manoah, Though thou detain me, I will not eat of thy bread: and if thou wilt offer a burnt offering, thou must offer it unto the Lord. Manoah knew not that he was an angel of the Lord.

This text requires a thoughtful reader to understand that if Manoah knew not that he was encountering an angel of the Lord, he *should* have known, just as his wife did. If we happen to miss this message, the text provides more signs of Manoah's inadequate understanding.

Manoah ignores the angel's recommendation that he, in gratitude for being advised about the coming birth of a son, offer a traditional burnt offering to the Lord. Instead, he asks more stupid questions:

> And Manoah said unto the angel of the Lord, What is thy name, that when thy sayings come to pass we may do thee honor? And the angel of the Lord said unto him, Why asketh thou thus after my name, seeing it is secret? So Manoah took a kid . . . and offered it on a rock unto the Lord; and the angel did wondrously; . . . . when the flame went up toward heaven from off the altar, the angel of the Lord ascended in the flame of the altar. And Manoah and his wife looked on it, and fell on their faces to the ground. But the angel of the Lord did no more appear to Manoah and his wife. Then Manoah knew that he was an angel of the Lord. And Manoah said unto his wife, We shall surely die, because we have seen God. But his wife said unto him, If the Lord were pleased to kill us he would not have received a burnt offering . . . at our hands, neither would he have shewed us all these things, nor would he . . . have told us such things as these.

A modern reader will not likely believe in the possibility of an angelic man of God, nor in the efficacy of burnt offerings, nor in a fantastical miracle concerning a human-appearing angel going up in smoke, but he should be able to catch the theme here. The ancient Hebrews were less interested in the reality of seeming miracles than in the difference between rational minds and idolatrous minds. After viewing what he took to be a demonstration of the man of

God's smoky power, Manoah falls to the ground in reverence. But he understands nothing. He thinks he's going to die. Only with thoughtful instruction can his rational wife set him straight.

The author of this story has crafted events so that at the beginning Manoah trots behind his rational wife, and he remains there to the end, unable to distinguish a *nazir* from an idolater. And neither could his son. They both lacked a mature executive function.

IV: MORE A BRUTE THAN A *NAZIR*

In this context we meet Samson, whose muscular strength did not serve him well. Though the Philistines feared him, they could outwit him, at a heavy price to be sure, but one that they probably thought worth paying. The Philistines unintentionally arranged matters so that in killing himself Samson also brought down the Philistine Temple on the heads of a multitude of Philistines. Nevertheless, these implacable enemies of Israel were left standing to fight further rounds against the troubling monotheists and their abstract God.

The ancient Hebrews, for whom Samson's story was composed, saw their ongoing struggles with the Philistines not simply as a war of conquest. More importantly, it was a fight for rationality, justice, and law, ideas that the Philistine idolaters could not understand or tolerate.

Unfortunately, the ancient Hebrews sometimes doubted their own capacity to grasp abstract values conveyed to them by an immaterial God. Even their *nazir*, Samson, repeatedly undermined himself by giving free rein to his inadequate executive function. Thus the case of Samson illustrated for the ancient Hebrews their own repeated failure to make appropriated choices. They recalled that their ancestors made a golden calf, so they were more interested in the flaws of their heroes than in the folly of their neighbors. The crudity of child sacrifice was easier to condemn than the degradation of their abstract values, which were and are, like the Hebrew God, not visible to the eye. Samson never could see his own frailties.

Even without a vocabulary for psychological impairment, the ancient Hebrews discerned that there is an observable kind of mind, featuring what is now called an impaired executive function, that regularly undermines the ability to compose a rational way to live.

The absence of a name for this inept behavior made it more difficult to discern it in oneself or in ones leaders. So it was left to skillful writers, like the author of Judges, to use narrative to convey ideas that can only be implied. A leader with a well-honed executive function, like Joshua or Deborah, had to be shown as succeeding in his or her well-conceived acts, and, on the other hand, those who foist devastation on themselves or on their community had to be rejected, be they king, judge, *nazir*, or a village idiot like Manoah.

Immediately after Manoah's wife instructs her husband on logical thinking, we learn in a compact narrative that Samson was born and grew, that the Lord blessed him, which unfortunately led him to act as if he understood nothing about being a *nazir*. In rapid sequence, Samson orders his parents to fetch him a Philistine woman who had caught his eye, marries her despite his parents' reasonable objections ("Is there never a woman among the daughters of thy brethren . . . that thou goest to take a wife of the uncircumcised Philistines?"}, slaughters a lion, returns to the lion's carcass to drink honey from a hive of bees that had set up a colony therein, invents a riddle based on his lion story, uses this riddle to bet that his friends cannot solve it, mistreats his new wife, which primes her to betray the secret of his riddle, loses his bet, gets angry, slays 30 Philistine men in Ashkelon, gives his wife to one of his companions, catches 300 foxes, attaches firebrands to their tales, then sets them free in Philistine fields, thus provoking the Philistines to burn Samson's perfidious ex-wife and her father.

Samson then defends himself against the Philistine vengeance that he should have expected. He finds an old jawbone of an ass, with which he kills another thousand Philistines. All this could be thought of as a kind of mania, but mania is episodic, often shifting back and forth between a variety of intensely driven pursuits and a calm, reasonable, and recognizable personality. Samson is never calm, never himself, never truly a *nazir*, never a mere womanizer, never a reliable soldier, always an exhibitionist, always in pursuit of the most recent fabrication of his immature executive function. His personality is constant only in that his frontal lobes are reliably unreliable.

With a busy, unpredictable schedule in his background, Samson illustrates behavior that is relevant to his role of a *nazir* only in the sense that it contains nothing but the opposite of what is expected. Nevertheless, Samson "judged Israel in the days of the Philistines 20 years."

We are not surprised when he continues to make the same kind of foolish mistakes. As soon as he goes into the Philistine land, he treats himself to an unnamed harlot, who unsuccessfully tries to learn the secret of his strength. Though Samson escapes from this dangerous harlot, matters become more problematic after he casts his eyes on the more seductive Delilah.

From then on, his luck runs out, as was usually the case for ancient Hebrew leaders with poor executive function, such as the psychotic King Saul. Thus, our writer's main purpose was not to stigmatize Philistine women but to caution the stiff-necked Hebrews about their risk of being easily seduced into dangerous irrationality.

Let us pick up the rampaging story of Samson at the beginning of Judges 16:

> Then went Samson to Gaza, and saw there an harlot and went in unto her. And it was told the Gazites, saying, Samson is come hither. And they compassed him in, and laid wait for him all night in the gait of the city, and they were quiet all the night,

saying, In the morning, when it is day, we shall kill him. And Samson . . . arose at midnight, and took the doors of the gate of the city, and the two posts and went away with them, bar and all, and put them on his shoulders, and carried them up to the top of an hill that is before Hebron. And it came to pass afterward, that he loved a woman in the valley of Sorek, whose name was Delilah.

Samson, with his great physical strength, pulled down and then hauled the heavy city gates of Gath up a mountain. But his mind was not as powerful. He repeats the same ridiculous behavior over and again, each time expecting a better result, just like other people with inadequate executive function.

Samson may seem insane on occasion, but he is not. Those with impaired executive function make inappropriate choices that can nevertheless be intelligently enacted; the insane usually enact bizarrely conceived, senseless mischief. Samson's attraction to eye-catching women, first the unnamed harlot and then Delilah, his seizing the opportunity to sip honey from the carcass of the lion he killed, his urge to kill a multitude of idolatrous Philistines, and his clever plan to use his muscular power to pull down the Philistine Temple on his own head cannot be said to be entirely senseless. But all his acts are inappropriate to his role as a *nazir*, and counter-productive to his supposed goal of freeing the Hebrews from Philistine assault.

In any case, Samson, while continuing to operate as a Judge, hooks up with Delilah, whose handlers have ordered her, just as they ordered Samson's previous harlot, to wheedle her man into divulging the secret of his strength; thus purrs Delilah:

> And she said unto him, How canst thou say, I love thee, when thy heart is not with me? Thou has mocked me these three times, and hast not told me wherein thy great strength lieth. And it came to pass, when she pressed him daily with her words, and urged him, so that his soul was vexed unto death; That he told her all his heart, and said unto her, There hath not come a razor upon my head; for I have been a Nazarite unto God from my mother's womb: if I be shaven, then my strength will from me, and will be like any other man. And when Delilah saw that he had told her all his heart . . . . she made him sleep upon her knees; and she called for a man, and she caused him to shave the seven locks of his head; and she began to afflict him, and his strength went from him. And she said, The Philistines be upon thee, Samson. And he awoke out of his sleep, and said, I will go out as at other times before, and shake myself. And he wist not that that the Lord was departed from him.

With a nice literary touch, our narrator notes Samson's inability to register God's having abandoned him. This failure resembles Manoah's inability to recognize the angelic quality of the man of God. Like father like son. Manoah and Samson both lack the capacity to weave a multiplicity of details together so that cogent thinking can emerge and effective action can follow.

Larger than the value of Samson's material hair is the value of the meaning of that hair. Somehow Samson believes that there are no real consequences of his having been shorn. He thinks that he can get up and "go out as at other times before and shake myself."

The Hebrew verb that the King-James Bible translates as "shake myself" is *anatser*, which is not reflexive but transitive. Given Samson's nature, he probably means that he is ready "to go out as at previous times and *overthrow* the Philistines." That is the meaning of the same Hebrew verb in Exodus 14:27, where God *overthrows* the Pharaoh's charioteers in the Red Sea. The King-James version of this verse about "shaking" himself reduces a pointed allusion to a trite morning stretch.

The Philistines possessed enough executive function to devise a plan to get Samson to betray himself, but not enough know-how to defend themselves from their captive's shrewd counter-attack. He tricks the boy who was managing him in the Philistine Temple into placing him in just the right position to pull down the Temple on the heads of the thousands there to honor their god, Dagon (whose name can be translated as Big Fish}.

The Hebrew reader of this story is of course meant to understand that Samson's true strength lies not in his hair, not in material things of any kind, not in his muscular body, but in his mind, in his dedication to his role as a *nazir*. Samson should have understood his obligation to help his people follow God's commands to be truthful, honest, and just.

Samson knows he has been ordered not to ever cut his hair, but he doesn't have the wherewithal to defend his hair or the Hebrew values for which it stands. He cannot even defend his life. Nevertheless, after he is shorn, he continues to believe that can act as a spiritual leader even when he is unable to register that God has already abandoned him.

Nor does Samson have any idea of what awaits him as a prisoner of the Philistines, even though he has been cruel to the Philistines with his vengeful slaughters, his lethal ass's jawbone, and his incendiary foxes. But perhaps this is not surprising in a man who lacks the executive function to guess what Delilah might have in store for him. He is surprised, at the conclusion of Judges 16, to learn what the Philistine bosses have planned for him while they drunkenly celebrate their god's victory over him. Immediately, the man who never saw clearly has his eyes gouged out, and:

> Then the lords of the Philistines gathered themselves together to offer a great sacrifice unto Dagon their god, and to rejoice: for they said, Our god hath delivered Samson our enemy into our hand. And when the people saw him, they praised their god. And it came to pass, when their hearts were merry, that they said, Call for Samson that he make us sport; and they . . . set him between the pillars. Samson said unto the lad that held him by the hand, Suffer me that I may feel the pillars whereupon the

house standeth, that I may lean upon them. Now the house was full of men and women; and all the Lords of the Philistines were there; and there were on the roof about three thousand men and women while Samson made sport. And Samson called unto the Lord, and said, O Lord God, remember me, I pray thee, and strengthen me, I pray thee, only this once, O God, that I may be at once avenged of the Philistines for my two eyes. And Samson took hold of the two middle pillars upon which the house stood, of the one with the right hand, and of the other with his left. And Samson said, Let me die with the Philistines. And he bowed himself with all his might; and the house fell on the lords and all the people therein. So the dead which he slew were more than they which he slew in his life. Then his brethren . . . buried him . . . in the burying place of Manoah his father.

This concluding passage of Judges 16 seals our *nazir*'s misuse of his strength. The ancient Hebrews demanded a great strength of virtue, not of muscle. Vengeance, in the Hebrew view, is not to be pursued, nor is violence. In his last words to his stiff-necked people, Moses reminds his congregants in Deuteronomy 32:35 that vengeance corrupts the soul and thus should remain in God's hands. Thus, the Lord says, "To me belongeth vengeance."

But Samson, unable to draw on the ancient wisdom of his people, dies with vengeance on his lips (the Hebrew word, *nakam*, "vengeance," is used in both Deuteronomy 32 and Judges 16). In violation of the Hebrew respect for life, Samson is proud to have killed more Philistines in dying than he ever killed by living. This is not an accomplishment appropriate for a *nazir*, and neither is Samson's enthusiasm for dying entangled in the arms of the Philistines: "Let my soul die with the Philistines."

Because he cannot properly evaluate his behavior, he becomes a negative example of both an ideal Hebrew Judge and an ideal citizen of the Hebrew Land. Appropriately, Samson is buried in his father's grave; the Hebrew word *kever* means *grave*, not "burying place," as the King-James translators would have it. That father and son were buried in the same grave reminds us that they lived in the same mental space. Even if we do not accept an essential difference between ethical monotheism and idolatry, we might still benefit from the Hebrew Bible's study of executive function, as well as the vast, ensuing literature on this subject.

CHAPTER SEVEN
AMBIVALENCE

I: THE HEBREWS STRADDLE

That the human mind is often driven in competing directions was common knowledge in the ancient world. In Homer's *Odyssey*, for example, after the fall of Troy, Odysseus is delayed for ten years while encountering one obstacle after another as he sails across a turbulent Mediterranean Sea, longing most of the time to get back to his Kingdom of Ithaca and his devoted wife, Penelope. But thrown into the arms of Circe, he shares her bed for a year, his passions divided. Aeneas suffers a similar division of loyalties in the *Aeneid*; he can barely be extracted from the lovely arms of Dido, despite his mission to found Rome.

But in these classic epics, ambivalent behavior was never thought to arise spontaneously within an individual's mind, nor did the idea of the mind yet have what Shakespeare calls "a local habitation and a name." Contradictory feelings and thoughts were attributed to intrusive gods with conflicting motives, such as the wise Athena and the unpredictable Poseidon. Because little was known about body's organs, how and where the gods meddled was never clear. Love was arbitrarily lodged in the heart, courage in the liver; the brain was terra incognita.

Nevertheless, for centuries ambivalent minds were recognized. Finally, careful observers of human behavior recognized the medical nature of ambivalence. Rather abruptly, psychological symptoms were seen as emanating from a disordered brain; Greek gods were no longer granted precedence. In the late Nineteenth century, Emil Kraeplin noted a pattern of irrational behavior in patients who shared similarly bizarre symptoms with other members of the same family. Kraeplin thought these patients suffered a genetic disease of the brain, which he called dementia praecox.

Eugen Bleuler soon corrected Kraeplin by pointing out that these patients do not suffer any form of slowly progressive dementia, such as Alzheimer's disease, but rather episodic attacks of a distinct set of four symptoms, later memorialized as Bleuler's four A's: disturbances of *affect*, *associations* of unrelated ideas, *ambivalence* (endorsing conflicting thoughts and feelings about the same entity), and *autism* (self-preoccupation). For Bleuler the brain was sometimes at odds with itself; he called this state *schizophrenia* (a divided *mind*).

Schizophrenia is now understood as a disease of the material brain, not the splitting of the still-abstract mind, but there is still truth in both Bleuler's and Freud's view that the mind as essentially in constant conflict with its different parts. The life spans of these two psychiatrists were virtually the same; born a year apart, they both died in 1939, having shared the authorship of Freud's first book, *On Hysteria*.

But Bleuler thought of ambivalence as a brain disease, and Freud, though trained as a neurologist, found it impossible to base his theories on the available neuroscience. His theory of ambivalence rested instead on the conflicting agencies of ego and id, wherever they might be in the brain.

Surprisingly, the writers of the *Tanach* also studied ambivalence according to the modern understanding of conflicting mental agencies. Even though they lacked the neuroscience of Bleuler and the psychoanalysis of Freud, they at least rejected the ancient "experts" of deep psychology, whom the *Tanach* calls *Yedoni*, that is, knowers or wizards, as in Leviticus 20:27. For these were equivalent to the proponents of child sacrifice, as described in Deuteronomy 18:9-11:

> When thou art come into the land which the Lord thy God giveth thee, thou shalt not learn to do after the abominations of those nations. There shall not be found among you any one that maketh his son or his daughter to pass through the fire, or useth divination or an observer of times [an astrologist],

or an enchanter or a witch. Or a charmer, or a consulter with familiar spirits, or a wizard, or a necromancer.

For the Ancient Hebrews, the most pressing psychological problem before them was their shaky ability to remain devoted to their rational Lord. They found themselves often attracted to the irrational beliefs of their idolatrous neighbors, barely able to cling to their monotheistic Torah. Even after being roundly chastised after fabricating the Golden Calf, for which they were punished with a plague just as bad as those foisted on Pharaoh, the unreliable Hebrews continued to straddle.

They thanked their Lord after safely crossing the Red Sea, singing joyfully in Exodus 15:1-2 as Pharaoh's men were drowning behind them:

> Then sang Moses and the children of Israel this song unto the Lord . . . saying, I will sing unto the Lord, . . . The Lord is my strength and song, and he is become my salvation: he is my God. I will prepare him a habitation; my father's God, and I will exalt him.

Nevertheless these grateful Hebrews remained attracted to the idolatrous customs of their neighbors, apparently not much disturbed by cognitive dissonance. Though modern readers may find little interest in the Hebrew God of miraculous salvation, they might be enlightened by the ancient

Hebrews' exploration of their near-fatal ambivalence, from which they have barely survived.

A good place to begin a discussion of the *Tanach*'s study of ambivalence is the story of Elijah's confrontation with the followers of King Ahab and Queen Jezebel. These mad and murderous usurpers of the Hebrew kingship enticed most of their citizens to abandon their Lord and enter the service of the god, Ba'al. The unreliable Hebrews then became of mixed minds, unable to distinguish the Lord from a lord.

Ahab and Jezebel had already assassinated the majority of the Lord's prophets, believing that it was easier to overthrow the Hebrew's invisible Lord if His visible prophets were also rendered invisible. Elijah, a rational man of God, did what he could to hide the remaining prophets in groups of fifty to a cave, with each cave close to a water source and supplied with food by Elijah himself.

This fairy-tale-like story becomes more dramatic when the Hebrew Lord stages a counter attack by imposing a drought to match the current drought of reason. Ahab is forced to send his still-righteous governor, Obadiah (Hebrew for Servant of God), to find Elijah, now in hiding. Obadiah does find Elijah, and he dutifully brings Ahab to the man who might be able to bring forth rain.

To assure that that readers of the story of Elijah's assault on Hebrew ambivalence does not rest on miracles but on reason, the author of I Kings 18:42-45 tells how Elijah rigs matters so that the natural coming of rain appears miraculous:

And Elijah went up to the top of Carmel . . . And said to his servant, Go up now, look at the sea. And he went up, and looked, and said, There is nothing. And he said, Go again seven times. And it came to pass at the seventh time, that he said, Behold, there ariseth a little cloud out of the sea, like a man's hand [Hebrew *kaf-eesh*, palm] . . . . And it came to pass in the meanwhile that the heaven was black with clouds and wind, and there was a great rain.

Elijah waits until there is a sign, a tiny cloud as small as a man's palm, that rain is already on the way before he sets his "miracle" in motion. Understanding that his people needed miracles to confirm, at least for a moment, everything they believed, Elijah realizes that he needs another miracle on Mount Carmel to end the reign of Ba'al, at least temporarily. And Elijah does deliver the miracle he needs, but this time the secret of the trick is not revealed, though the previous miracle alerts the reader to the likelihood of stagecraft. In any case, miracle is not the point of Elijah's staged show.

The text is careful to signal that Elijah's powers are not miraculous but the product of reason; he aims to prove that the powers of Ba'al, as well as the beliefs of his followers, are laughable. This narrative, told with a fine literary sensibility, is one of several texts in *Tanach* (as we shall see) that use humor to make a dead-serious point.

The point is that that the priests of Ba'al are ridiculous, deserving of Elijah's mockery, and so are the idol-worshipping Hebrews. They continue to halt "between two opinions," as we see in I Kings 17:25-41:

> And it came to pass, when Ahab saw Elijah, that Ahab said unto him, Art thou he that troubleth Israel? And he answered, I have not troubled Israel; but thou, and thy father's house, in that ye have forsaken the commandments of the Lord, and thou has followed Ba'alim [false gods]. Now therefore send, and gather to me all Israel unto mount Carmel, and the prophets of Baal, four hundred and fifty, and the prophets of the grove four hundred, which eat at Jezebel's table. . . . So Ahab sent unto all the children of Israel, and gathered the prophets together unto mount Carmel. And Elijah came unto all the people, and said, How long halt ye [Hebrew *pesachim*, second-person plural of *pesach*, hesitate, or straddle] between two opinions? If the Lord be God follow him: but if Ba'al, then follow him. And the people said not a word.

The Hebrew word that the King-James translate as "halt" is *pesach*, the same Hebrew word used for the name of the Passover Holiday, and the same word used to describe what God's angel of death did while hesitating over Hebrew household while on the way to destroying the first-born of Egypt. Though the Jewish homes are clearly marked via an elaborate ritual involving the spreading of sacrificial blood on every Jewish doorpost, the destroying angel nevertheless hovers over these clearly-identified homes. Why not allow the punitive angel to soar over safe Jewish homes without stopping above them? Why use the ambiguous verb, *pesach*, when the clearer verb *ahvar*, translated as "pass through," has already been used in the very same verse, Exodus 12:23:

> For the Lord will pass through [*ahvar*] to smite the Egyptians; and when he seeth the blood upon the lintel, and on the two side posts, the Lord will pass over [*pesach*] the door, and will not suffer the destroyer to come in unto your houses to smite you.

But *pesach* does not mean *pass-over*, nor does it mean *halt*. Onkelos, who in the early second-century translated the *Tanach* from Hebrew into Aramaic, gives the Aramaic equivalent "spare" for what God did over Jewish homes; but that is not quite the right word, either. The reason "the destroyer" pauses over Hebrew homes is likely because the headstrong slaves, the makers of the Golden-Calf, have still not broken away from their chronic ambivalence. Thus the destroyer had to think a bit about what he should do to the stiff-necked Hebrews.

P*esach* also means "to limp," and we shall soon see that at their best the Hebrews barely manage to limp way from their ambivalent quest for freedom from slavery. By Eijah's reckoning, the children of Israel straddled between two opinions, ambivalent about their unique heritage, just as they were dubious about their Promised Land even before they occupied it. And now, confronted by Elijah for their chronic straddling, they have nothing to say. For to answer

Elijah they would have to choose either the One God, or the multiple gods that were all called Ba'al. They remained silent, for they had no answer ("the people said not a word").

Because of their habitual ambivalence, Elijah designs a test to induce the chosen people to stop wavering and choose wisely:

> And Elijah said unto the prophets of Baal, Choose you one bullock for yourselves, and dress it first, for ye are many; and call on the names of your gods, but put not fire under. And they took the bullock given them, and they dressed it, and called on the name of Baal from morning even unto noon, saying, O Baal, hear us. But there was no voice, nor any that answered. And they leaped upon [Hebrew *pesach* = hovered over] the altar which [they themselves] made. And it came to pass at noon, that Elijah mocked them, and said, Cry aloud: for he is a god; either he is talking, or he is pursuing, or he is in a journey, or peradventure he sleepeth, and must be awakened. And they cried aloud, and cut themselves after their manner with knives and lancets, till the blood ran out of them. . . . And Elijah took twelve stones according to the number of the sons of Jacob . . . And with the stones he built an altar in the name of the Lord: and he made a trench about the altar . . . . And he put the wood in order and cut the bullock in pieces, and laid it on the wood, and said, and said, Fill four barrels with water, and pour it on the wood. And . . . a second time . . . . And they did it a third time . . . .

And it came to pass at the time of the evening sacrifice, that Elijah the prophet came near and said,
. . . Hear me, O Lord, hear me that this people may
know that thou are the Lord god and that thou has
turned their heart back. Then the fire of the Lord
fell and consumed the burnt-sacrifice, and the wood
and the stones . . . . And when all the people saw
it, they fell on their faces: and they said, The Lord,
he is the God; the Lord, he is the God, the Lord,
he is the God.

Under the influence of Elijah, the Hebrews on Mount
Carmel gave up their straddling between idolatry and monotheism. But this was possible only because Elijah succeed-
ed, via a staged "miracle," in mocking the idiocy of idolatry and celebrating the rationality of monotheism. Modern
readers of this extravaganza would not likely be persuaded
that divine fire actually descended from heaven to consume
thoroughly-soaked meat, wood, and stones.

But they might believe that it is foolish to follow the
absurd self-slashing of Ba'al's devotees (they "cut themselves
after their manner with knives and lancets"), especially if a
rational alternative is offered. And modern skeptics would
certainly laugh with Elijah as he teased the Hebrew idolaters to yell louder, for their god might be sleeping, hunting,
or on a journey, somewhere distant, very distant.

Precisely because self-mutilation is an irrational rejection of the Creator's work, this barbaric custom was specifically banned from the Promised Land. Thus Leviticus

19:28: "Thou shall not make any cuttings in thy flesh." This self-destructive primitiveness alone should have been sufficient to warn Elijah's Mount-Carmel Hebrews against the whole line of idolatrous nonsense. But though these students did learn a bit about the folly of their ambivalence, their persistent stubbornness rendered them vulnerable to further lapses. And that is what they did, over and again.

The Passover Holiday celebrates freedom from physical slavery, cognitive slavery, and spiritual slavery. We might, then, consider abandoning the English name and cleave to Passover's Hebrew name. *Pesach* celebrates the limping away from ambivalence to the challenging freedom of rationality.

II: The Liberated Jews Continued to Straddle, And So Did Pharaoh

The narrative of the Exodus from Egypt focuses not only on the divided loyalties of the Hebrews but also, surprisingly, on the revelation that the all-powerful Pharaoh was ambivalent, too. This parallel takes us out of the local realm of the Israelites into a serious discussion about how human ambivalence in general compromises our ability to live well and choose wisely.

Waking to the widespread death of the firstborn caused by the tenth plague, Pharaoh pleads not for relief from his Egyptian gods, but for a blessing from the Hebrew God:

And the Pharaoh rose up in the night, he, and all his servants, and all the Egyptians; and there was a great cry in Egypt, for there was not a house where there were not one dead. And he called for Moses and Aaron by night, and said, Rise up and get you forth from among my people, both you and the children of Israel; and go, serve the Lord, as you have said. . . and be gone; and bless me, also.

And this is not the first time Pharaoh has begged for a blessing from the God of the Hebrews. While in the midst of previous plagues, Pharaoh usually negotiated with Moses about how far and with whom the Hebrew troublemaker might take the Jews into the desert to celebrate their rituals, whatever those might be. In general, Pharaoh was not interested in God or gods but in tight control of his slaves. But during the eighth plague, when locusts cover the entire land, Pharaoh reveals, in Exodus 10:14-17, that he is now taking Moses' God seriously:

> And the locusts went up over all the land of Egypt, and rested on all the coasts of Egypt: very grievous were they; before them there were no such locusts as they, neither after them shall be such. For they covered the face of the whole earth, so the land was darkened through all the land of Egypt. Then Pharaoh called for Moses and Aaron in haste; and he said, I have sinned against the Lord thy God, and against you. Now therefore forgive, I pray thee, my sin only this once, that he take away from me this death only.

This narrative may seem to be a hyperbolic fable about monster locusts so thick that they darkened the entire land of Egypt. But it is certainly not meant that way, though a modern reader might take it so. The assertion that this overwhelming plague of locusts had never been seen before and will never be seen again gives the story an otherworldly quality, a metaphysical sense that the darkness is not the literal shadow of locusts but the darkness of idolatry, a mental fog.

Though the ancient Egyptians designed their pyramids with a small window at the summit so that every embalmed Pharaoh's immortal soul might eventually fly up to his star, those corpses are either still where they were laid in the pyramid's hollow center, or they were removed by ancient grave-robbers. A part of Pharaoh's mind seemed to know that his god was a sham, and this leads him to lurch toward the Hebrew God.

That the Pharaoh himself craves a blessing from the Hebrew God is likely meant not as a nod to a possible convert but as another warning to the recalcitrant Hebrews who often turned from one god or another.

Even the preceding Pharaoh, he who lifted Joseph into eminence, suddenly acknowledges in Genesis 41:39 that the wisdom of the Hebrew interpreter of dreams stems from the Hebrew God, and from no other: "Forasmuch as God hath shewed thee all this there is none so discreet and wise as thou art."

The ambivalent Pharaohs changed their minds often. Like all those who suffer ambivalence, Moses' Pharaoh reveals his protean mind, as we see in Exodus 14:5, where he suddenly decides to recall the fleeing Hebrews, a decision with a fatal consequence for him and his charioteers alike. This, too, is a reminder to the Hebrews that ambivalence has a price:

> And it was told the King of Egypt that the people fled: and the heart of Pharaoh and his servants were turned against the people, and they said, Why have we done this, that we have let Israel go from us? And he made ready his chariot and he took his people with him.

That God hardened Pharaoh's heart to direct his rash decision-making does not mean that Pharaoh would have acted more rationally had God not meddled. We are not in the genre of a Greek epic or a Greek tragedy. No gods are invited, including the Hebrew God. We are in a Hebrew tragedy, where a divided human mind is the villain. The point is that when ambivalence is the problem, it is frozen in its fluctuating state, difficult to moderate, as the Hebrews demonstrate time and again. God did not harden Pharaoh's heart but let it be.

Every modern psychotherapist has noted the truth of Freud's remark that symptoms are not problems but solutions, and thus difficult to dissolve. In our story, God hardens Pharaoh's heart only in the sense that he leaves it frozen in a fixed pattern, ricocheting between the plague of idolatry and Hebrew reason. Idolatry is a solution to the problem of being alone in an eternal fight against the slings and arrows of outrageous fortune; one is not likely to forsake one's favorite god of metal or wood for an invisible, incomprehensible God of Creation.

Millennia ago, the Hebrews noted that they, too, were up against a problem so large that even the Pharaoh could not solve it. There was no good reason to turn to Ba'al for help, but there would always be Hebrews who would give it a try. Similarly, there was no good reason for Pharaoh to chase the bothersome Hebrews into the Red Sea, but off he went. For irrational Idolatry is not easy to forgo. What makes clinging to idols easier for otherwise reasonable men is the capacity to hide the irrationality of idolatry in a blanket of ambivalence.

Perhaps that is why, early in the Torah, we find the story of Rachel stealing her father's household idols, hiding them under her donkey's saddle-blankets as she left for Canaan with her new husband, Jacob. She did use her Hebraic intelligence by concocting a fiction for her father that she couldn't rise from her donkey because she was menstruating, thus hiding both her little idols and her own ambivalence. Why else might she want to pack these mini comfort-animals?

III: Balaam Might or Might Not Curse

We see an example of ambivalence in action in the story of Balak and Balaam, where we also find a good deal of humor.

As the Hebrews began their conquest of the Promised Land, they soon ran into the expected opposition, but the stories about their conquests are not of the usual military type. Neither tactics nor strategies are discussed, and we learn nothing about available armaments. Rather the psychology of Balak and Balaam figure prominently, and though their complex story concerns the Hebrews only indirectly, it tells us much about the psychology of both the Hebrews and their enemies.

Let us begin in Numbers 22 with Balak's fear of the children of Israel, who are now surrounding him after destroying the Amorites. This looming calamity forces Balak to plea to Balaam not for military assistance but for effective cursing:

> And the children of Israel set forward, and pitched in the plains of Moab . . . . And Balak, son of Zippor, saw all that Israel had done to the Amorites. And Moab was sore afraid of the people, because they were many: and Moab was distressed because of the children of Israel. And Moab said, ... Now shall this company lick up all that are around us, as the ox licketh up the grass of the field. And Balak the son of Zippor was King of the Moabites at that time. He sent messengers therefore unto

Balaam, . . . saying, Behold, there is a people come out of Egypt: behold, they cover the face of the earth, and they abide over against me: Come now therefore, curse me this people; for they are too mighty for me . . . . for I wot that he whom thou blesseth is blessed and whom thou cursest is cursed.

We should note that Balak is twice mentioned here as the son of Zippor, which in Hebrew means *Bird*, a name that the Hebrews would recognize as belonging to Horus and many other feathered gods of Egypt, who were deified because of their avian capacity to fly up into the heavens. Balak, the son of Big Bird, is looking, from his perspective, for salvation from a master of curses who knows nothing about military combat. What counts is cursing, as in the idolatrous world of voodoo.

Balak doesn't realize that in praising Balaam's expert capacity to curse, he alludes to the Hebrew God's promise to Abraham in Genesis 12:3, "I will bless them that bless thee, and curse him that curseth thee; and in thee shall all families of the earth be blessed." Balak thus sets up a conflict that Balaam will be asked to resolve. Will Balaam follow the dictates of Balak to curse whom the Hebrew God has blessed, or will he follow the Hebrew God's promise to bless the Hebrews and those who bless them?

And this is where the story gets complicated, for Balaam tries to find a way to praise and curse, becoming an emblem of Hebrew ambivalence. By viewing Hebrew ambivalence projected into the mind of an intelligent non-Hebrew, the Hebrews might perceive their own duplicity, but maybe not.

When Balak's diplomatic emissaries arrive with Balak's request in the court of Balaam, the divided man begs permission to think the matter over; and by morning he seems to have found the right answer:

> Balaam rose up in the morning, and said unto the princes of Balak, Get you into your land: for the Lord refuseth to give me leave to go with you.

Since this is a story about ambivalence, the Lord's refusal to support Balak's request does not bring the matter to an end:

> And Balak sent yet again princes, more and more honorable than they. And they came to Balaam and said to him . . . Let nothing, I pray thee, hinder thee from coming unto me. For I will promote thee unto very great honour, and I will do whatsoever thou sayest unto me: come therefore, I pray thee, curse me this people. And Balaam answered . . . . If Balak would give me his house full of silver and gold, I cannot go beyond the word of the Lord my God, to do less or more.

This, too, would seem to put an end to the matter. But Balaam changes course again, this time with an illogical "therefore":

Now therefore, I pray you, tarry ye this night, that I may know what the Lord will say unto me more. And God came unto Balaam at night, and said unto him, If the men come to call thee, rise up, and go with them; but yet the word which I shall say unto thee, that shall you do.

The story would not continue to hang in suspense like this, with no clear resolution of Balaam's dilemma, if ambivalence were not the theme of the story. Will Balaam follow the deity he calls "the Lord my God," or will he follow the urging of Balak and the opportunity to enhance his wealth and reputation? The reason that the Lord Himself prolongs the suspense here must be to emphasize Hebrew ambivalence. If there were no such issue among the Hebrews, this complicated story would not likely have found a place in the Torah.

So Balaam gets on his donkey and goes to Balak in Moab. He quickly finds himself in the strangest part of this story, which happens to be another example of the *Tanach* using humor to make a serious point:

Balaam rose up in the morning and saddled his ass, and went with the princes of Moab. And God's anger was kindled [Hebrew *va'yechar af*] because he went: and the angel of the Lord stood in the way for an [as an] adversary against him. Now he was riding upon his ass, and his two servants were with him. And the ass saw the angel of the Lord standing in the way, and his sword drawn in his hand:

and the ass turned aside out of the way, and went into the field: and Balaam smote the ass to turn her into the way. But the angel of the Lord stood in a path of the vineyards, a wall being on this side, and a wall on that side. And when the ass saw the angel of the Lord, she thrust herself unto the wall, and crushed Balaam's foot against the wall: and he smote her again. And the angel of the Lord went further, and stood in a narrow place, where was no way to turn . . . . And when the ass saw the angel of the Lord, she fell down under Balaam: and Balaam's anger was kindled [Hebrew *va'yechar af*], and he smote her again.

That the donkey can see the angel of the Lord when Balaam cannot is not simply humorous but tells us that something is wrong with Balaam's perception. And that the same word is used to describe both God's anger with Balaam and Balaam's anger with his donkey tells us that there is something wrong with Balaam's ridiculous idea that he might be able to overrule the God of the Hebrews. Balaam does not understand what his donkey understands, and he has no understanding of how he has provoked his Lord's anger.

Though Balaam is not himself an ancient Hebrew, he nevertheless calls the Hebrew Lord "my God," and thus becomes a proxy for the ambivalent Hebrews. Balaam simply cannot comprehend that as a devotee of the Hebrew God he has no business engaging with Balak.

The ancient rabbis had a good deal of trouble under-standing why God approved Balaam's visit to Balak . Even God's carefully limited conditions for this visit seemed besides the point. The highly-respected Twelfth century commentator, Rashi, proposed that perhaps God was giving the otherwise righteous Balaam a chance to earn a living while finding a way to avoid a true cursing of Israel, but this, and other similar commentaries, make little sense. That an evil is small does not justify its partial enactment.

A more likely interpretation is that the author of the story wants to demonstrate the extent of Balaam's foolish ambivalence. Why should Balaam quarrel with his don-key and go all the way to Moab simply to repeat himself? Ambivalence is widespread among Jews and gentiles, who cannot undo their duplicity no matter where they take it.

The story goes on to show how ridiculous an attempt to override the obvious can be. When Balaam finally arrives in Balak's court, the frustrated King marches Balaak to three idolatrous shrines, each on a different hilltop, and each fit-ted with seven altars to support Balaam's cursing. One after another, Balaam's attempts to curse Israel fail under a cloud of humor. Balaam keeps consulting his Lord, and on each occasion the Lord orders Balaam to praise Israel in poems so beautiful that some of them still appear in the daily lit-urgy of the Jews. Perhaps the humor of witnessing Balak's repetitively futile labor might bring the Hebrews' ambiva-lent toying with idolatry to a close, but of course it does not, and cannot, given the stiff-necked nature of the people.

CHAPTER EIGHT
WISDOM

I: WISE SOLOMON

King Solomon has long been celebrated in the West for his wisdom. But what, exactly, do we find wise about this king's understanding?

Was Solomon wiser than the all-wise Athena at mastering the principles of ethical living? The Hebrew cognoscenti would not find it difficult to answer this question. Once they understood how the ancient Greeks thought of their mythical goddess, they would find her repulsive.

Her birth occurred under the usual auspices of meddling gods, who on this occasion were particularly vicious. Athena was Zeus' daughter, conceived by his wife, Metis, the Titan goddess of good counsel. Zeus then learned that if Metis bore a male, he would overthrow his father. So

Zeus swallowed Metis. Then he surprisingly developed a severe headache, which was relieved by having chimeric Hephaestus, half man and half serpent, crack open his skull with an ax. Out popped a fully grown Athena, wearing military garb, thus prepared to be a goddess of victory and many other arts, including spinning, weaving, flute playing (though she never played the flute), and other crafts in the line of Cain. But her wisdom lay not in the realm of philosophy or theology but in military strategy; and that was best demonstrated in the *Iliad* by her striking Ajax with madness as she busied herself on the battlefield of the Trojan War.

The ancient Greeks also installed Athena as the goddess of their chief city, naming it after her so that they might benefit from the salutary power of this wise goddess. She would foster education, science and philosophy. But even Athena was not wise enough to keep Athenians sufficiently informed. They needed their oracles, for without them they would be unprepared to confront raw and unpredictable life. Mortals were by definition unable to master themselves or their destiny.

In the case of Oedipus, the oracles did manage matters so that Oedipus was able to discover what was already in his own mind, his own memory, and his own fate. Freud, who was looking for support for his controversial ideas, claimed, somewhat disingenuously, that his discoveries agreed with what ancient poets like Sophocles already knew: human beings are driven by their memories. For Freud, wisdom about how to live derived from an understanding of ones own mind.

Solomon's wisdom is often said to be in the realm of this modern view of a wise mind, and so it was, but with a Hebraic difference. The *Tanach* eschews the whole world of Greek mythology, with its stories of ax-wielding, chimeric obstetricians delivering a full-grown female warrior. Although the *Tanach* from all appearances seems to accept Socrates' claim in Plato's *Apology of Socrates* that an unexamined life is not worth living, the Hebrew Bible carries out its version of self-examination under the canopy of ethical monotheism.

Let us consider the most famous example of Solomon's wisdom, which appears in I Kings 3:16-28. We will find that King Solomon was wise because he understood psychology; and then, afterwards, he was not so wise because he was not the master of his own mind.

Only the ability to understand the mind permits one to distinguish reason from delusion, justice from kangaroo chicanery, truth from folly, and, in short, monotheism from idolatry. Thus the author of Solomon's story focuses on the wise King's understanding of psychology:

> Then there came two women, that were harlots [or *innkeepers*], unto the king, and stood before him. And the one woman said, O my lord, I and this woman dwell in one house; and I was delivered of a child with her in the house. And it came to pass the third day after I was delivered, that this woman

was delivered also: and we were together; there was no stranger in the house, save we two in the house. And the woman's child died in the night because she overlaid it. And she arose at midnight, and took my son from beside me, while thine handmaid slept, and laid it in her bosom, and laid her dead child in my bosom. And when I rose in the morning to give my child suck, behold it was dead: but when I had considered it in the morning, behold it was not my son, which I did bear. And the other woman said, Nay; but the living is my son and the dead is thy son. And this said, No; but the dead is thy son and my son is the living.

Now, if one takes a legalistic view of these harlots' conflicting stories, there are, as usual, two sides. Each lady presents her case, each told in a different way, neither of them convincing. The first witness repeats herself ("in one house," "with her in the house," "no stranger in the house," "save we two in the house"). She seems nervous rather than enraged. She not only talks too much, but knows too much. How could she know that her rival "overlaid" her baby? New mothers do sometimes smother their babies by rolling over onto them, but that is not the only cause of neonatal death, even in ancient Israel.

And how does the complainant know that the kidnapper laid the stolen baby "in her bosom"? This is not the only way of sleeping with a baby in ancient Israel; in fact, the stolen baby in question was taken, according to the complainant herself, "from beside me." If this first witness were truly sleeping, how did she know where he was put after he was stolen? And how did she know exactly where her baby was sleeping with her without knowing that he was dead? Further, it would be virtually impossible to steal a baby sleeping besides his sleeping mother, for new mothers are hyper-vigilant. And, finally, we might ask why the first witness slips in a pleasing self-reference right in the middle of her description of her baby's theft: "And she arose at midnight, and took my son from beside me, *while thine handmaid slept.*" Is this not an attempt to sweet-talk the king into giving his handmaid special consideration?

Witness number two, the "other woman," does not have much to say for herself. Is this because she is a frightened thief? Or, is she stunned into near-silence by having her living baby shamelessly stolen from her by a fast-talking harlot? In ancient Israel, according the medieval commentator, Rashi, harlots were known to mask their houses of ill-repute as inns (see Joshua 2:1). If we are indeed dealing with harlots, how much can we believe either of these bereaved souls? Is this not a proverbial case of "she says, she says"? What is to be done?

Enter King Solomon. According to the details of this story, the legal dilemma posed to him approaches the insoluble. The wisdom that Solomon uses to solve the insoluble is not a clever legal argument but a ploy to apply his understanding of psychology:

> Then said the king. The one saith, This is my son that liveth, and thy son is dead: and the other

saith, Nay, but thy son is the dead, and my son is living. And the king said, Bring me a sword. And they brought a sword before the King. And the king said, Divide the living child in two, and give half to the one, and half to the other. Then spake the woman [the first witness] whose living child was unto the king, for her bowels yearned upon her son, and said, O my lord, give her the living child, and in no wise slay it. But the other said, Let it be neither mine or thine, but divide it. Then the king answered and said, Give her the living child, and in no wise slay it: she is the mother thereof.

The King allows no cross-examination of the witnesses, no lawyerly queries about problematic areas of the innkeepers' testimonies, for Solomon's wisdom does not lie in that quarter. More important than any law, or any testimony, is the King's understanding that a natural mother would never permit her son to be slaughtered, but an imposter of a mother just might.

On this occasion, Solomon's stratagem works well, but it is not as wise as it is reputed to be. With a quiet hint the author of this story identifies the true mother even *before* Solomon sees the effect of his command to divide the baby. Here is the telling phrase again:

And the king said, Divide the living child in two, and give half to the one, and half to the other. Then spake the woman [the first witness] whose living child was unto the king.

Our narrator reveals that the first witness, even before she responds to Solomon's command to divide the child, is the mother of the "living child," who is now on Solomon's lap.

If the appropriate outcome has already been determined, something more important than the clever crafting of a legal trap must be at stake, which is actually given in the story's conclusion:

> And all Israel heard of the judgment which the king had judged: and they feared [showed *awe* for] the king: and they saw that the wisdom of God was in him, to do judgment [i.e., *justice*].

If the author of this story wanted his readers to admire Solomon's legal acumen, he presumably would have had Solomon explore the holes in the first witnesses testimony, and he would not have arranged his story so that Solomon's clever ploy, which was designed to have a truth-revealing effect on the mothers, had a more important effect on "all Israel." What the Children of Israel "saw" in Solomon's ruling was "that the wisdom of God was in him to do judgment." There is no mention here of any public admiration for Solomon's clever legal maneuver or his understanding of psychology.

This story is aimed at all those ancient Hebrews whose psychology often misled them into the realm of idolatry and harlotry. In this story, the true basis of Solomon's reputation for wisdom is his capacity to earn the praise of all

Israel. Yes, he possesses an understanding of the psychology of mothers and innkeepers, but more importantly he has a deep understanding of the ancient Israelites themselves, who often behaved exactly like harlots in a "whoredom," as Hosea taught in his poetic prophecy.

From the Hebrew point of view, the capacity to rise above the inanities of idolatry to embrace the God of ethical monotheism rested mainly on a deep knowledge of how the mind works. There are righteous, life sustaining states of mind, and there are destructive states of mind. According to the wisdom of the *Tanach*, only a community devoted to a rational and just God can live a rational and just life.

II: SOLOMON'S WISE PROVERBS

According to a longstanding tradition, The Book of Proverbs was composed by Solomon himself. However this may be, we find in this collection further insights into what the ancient Hebrews considered true wisdom. The Book is introduced in this way:

> The proverbs of Solomon, the son of David, king of Israel: to know wisdom and instruction; to perceive the words of understanding; to receive the instruction of wisdom, justice, and judgment into equity. . . . The wise man shall hear, and will increase learning; and a man of understanding shall attain unto wise counsels: To understand a proverb, and the interpretation; the words of the wise and their dark [i.e., deep] sayings.

Here, the King-James translators capture the Hebrew essence of wisdom, which is not a thing but an abstraction, a capacity to see more deeply into the nature of things. By increasing his learning, a man "shall attain unto wise counsel," which anticipates by 2500 years the recommendations of Sir Francis Bacon in his *The Advancement of Learning*.

Sir Francis, as was mentioned earlier, borrowed the Hebrew abstract idea of an idol to catalogue the four kinds of "idols" that distract mankind from the pursuit of wisdom. As in the Hebrew Bible, these four idols were not literal things but representations of foolish distractions from the advancement of learning. One might hearken to the blathering of one's Tribe, which includes the entire tribe of humanity, or follow the moronic follies of ones narrow-minded associates in a local Cave, or one might abide by the ever-changing hucksterism in the current Market of opinion, or one can dumbly applaud the locally-prevailing follies in a provincial Theater of ideas.

Sir Francis' emblems of the Tribe, Cave, Market, and Theater serve well as a summary of the foolish distractions that misled the Children of Israel. These vacillating Hebrews acknowledged in story after story that they were often lured away from their rational Lord, and so they also undertook a mature investigation into the question of on what basis could they justify the choice of the God of Israel, and thus reject the many gods named Ba-al. They of course did not consider the choice of making no choice at all, probably because atheism was nowhere seen as a possibility in the ancient world. One could curse the gods, but one could not deny their existence.

From the time of Abraham, the Hebrews came to understand that they could choose one of many competing local gods or the One God of their forefathers. To choose this invisible God required a well-honed capacity to think deeply in abstract terms, a state of mind that we can call wisdom.

Those in the school of concrete thinking cannot interpret a proverb, for they cannot understand that a proverb requires an interpretation. Similarly, one cannot understand the value of a law without the capacity to understand the nature of value and the value of law. The Hebrews did understand, at least some of the time, that truth and value were abstract ideas, whose meanings were not obvious, nor were the commands of their invisible God to His people. Not even apparent miracles like manna or the splitting of the Red Sea had much effect on this obtuse people. In fact the miracles in Genesis served more as a literary device to portray the obliviousness of the stiff-necked Israelites than as a proof of God's power.

Hebraic wisdom, its necessity and its perversions, is the main focus of King Solomon's collection of proverbs, which are often opaque, requiring wisdom to understand the wisdom therein. A mastery of abstract thinking is required to distinguish wisdom from perversion, which, in Proverbs 2:10-17, are personified as "Discretion vs. "the Evil Man" and "the Strange Woman":

When wisdom entereth into thine heart [i.e., mind] and knowledge is pleasant unto thy soul; Discretion shall preserve thee, understanding shall keep thee: To deliver thee from the way of the evil man, . . . who leaves the paths of uprightness to walk in the ways of darkness; . . . [and] delivers thee from the strange woman, even from the stranger who flattereth with her strange words.

Without possessing wisdom at the outset, it is difficult to follow this argument about the abstract idea of "Discretion." One aspect of discretion is its power to save one from an emblematic "evil man," presumably a god like Ba'al, and from a "strange woman," presumably someone like Delilah, who "flattereth with her strange words."

Evaluating a patient's capacity for metaphorical thinking is actually part of the modern neurological and psychiatric method of evaluating patients. We may, for example, ask a troubled patient a question like this: "What do people mean when they say, 'People who live in glass houses shouldn't throw stones?'" A patient who handles metaphorical thought easily will answer, "People who are vulnerable to criticism shouldn't criticize," or, on further thinking, the patient might add, "People who are physically weak shouldn't start fights."

In contrast, a person who cannot understand metaphoric thought might say, as one of my patients did say, "If you live in a nice place, you shouldn't mess it up." Asked to explain his thinking, the young man said, "If you live in a nice place like a house with a fantastic view through large windows, you shouldn't throw stones all over the carpet."

Those who remain slaves to literalism, without the capacity to think abstractly, will find it impossible to achieve wisdom. They will blindly turn to "foreign women" without realizing that the term "foreign women" is a metaphor for embracing foolish ideas, such as idolatrous beliefs. They cannot work with metaphors, proverbs, and poetry, all of which are included in the Hebrew Bible, with a spotlight focused particularly on David's psalms and Solomon's proverbs.

III: Proverbs 31 Properly Perceived

Proverbs 31, called "*Eshet Chayil*" ("woman of valor" in Hebrew) begins with a plea for clear-headedness, for without this capacity wisdom is impossible. Men are who they are, their minds easily clouded, not only by lascivious women like Delilah, but by alcohol and other mental intoxicants, such as the many false promises of idolatry.

The *Tenach* means no literal disparagement of women by personifying idolatry as a woman, for the Hebrew word for idolatry is *avoda zara*, a feminine noun, just as *idolâtrie* is the feminine noun for idolatry in French. Similarly, wisdom is also personified in Hebrew as a woman; the Hebrew noun for wisdom is the feminine *chochma*, just as the French noun for wisdom is the feminine noun, *sagesse*.

To contrast the many ways of being seduced away from rational belief, the author of Proverbs 31, after warning about loose women and alcohol, turns to an idealized woman who masters all trades, all skills, local and international. She is a mistress of shipping, able to bring in food from afar, a talented weaver, an expert enologist, a real-estate mogul, and able to judge the value of merchandise. Unlike idolatrous women, she is virtuous, and her price is above rubies; her husband "doth safely trust in her." When she "girdeth her loins with strength, and strengtheth her arms," she is also like Athena, the goddess of military strategy, who "girdeth her loins with strength" when necessary, as we are told in Proverbs 31:10-25:

> Who can find a virtuous woman? For her price is far above rubies. . . . She seeketh wool and flax, and worketh willingly with her hands. She is like the merchants' ships; she bringeth her food from afar. She riseth also when it is still dark, and giveth meat to her household, and a portion to her maidens. She considereth a field and buyeth it; with the fruit of her hand she planteth a vineyard. She girdeth her loins with strength, and strengtheneth her arms. She perceiveth that her merchandise is good: her candle goeth out not at night. . . . She is not afraid of snow for her household: for all her household are clothed with scarlet. She maketh herself coverings of tapestry; her clothing is silk and purple. . . . She maketh fine line, and selleth it; and delivereth girdles unto the merchant. Strength and honour are her clothing; and she shall rejoice in time to come.

No actual woman could possibly manage all these skills and virtues, but anyone who wants to accomplish *any* of these abilities must master the wisdom of Solomon in its early form, before he degraded it.

Here is a bit of the introduction to Proverbs 31, which is about the power of abstract, Hebraic wisdom:

> Give not thy strength unto women, nor thy ways to that which destroys kings. . . . It is not for kings to drink wine; . . . Lest they drink, and forget the law, and pervert the judgment of any of the afflicted . . . . Open thy mouth, judge right-eously and plead the cause of the poor and needy . . . . Many daughters have done virtuously, but thou excellest them all. Favor is deceitful, and beauty is in vain: but a woman that feareth the Lord, she shall be praised.

It is certainly a shame that this personification of Hebraic wisdom is reduced to a tribute to the individual lady of every Jewish home on the eve of Sabbath. Though this custom is lovely, it misses the essence of the proverb. For what it celebrates is not an actual lady but an abstract idea, the wisdom of a rational system of belief that values ethical achievement. No single woman, no matter her piety, her intelligence, her skills, or her business acumen could lit-erally live up to Solomon's hymn to Judaic wisdom.

But every woman and every man does have the capacity to guide civilization in the right direction. Not until Imma-nuel Kant took up a formal analysis of abstract reasoning in the late Eighteenth century did the West improve on the wisdom of Solomon's Proverb 35. We will return to Kant, whose Hebrew name means, "God is with us."

IV: Solomon Betrays His Own Wisdom

What are we to do with those who, mired in literalism, cannot distinguish God from an idol, wisdom from clever manipulation, justice from perversion, a parakeet from a parable? Surprisingly, the story of Solomon is not only about his wisdom but also about his failure to be steadfast in wisdom. He is his own counter example.

Chapter 11 of I Kings begins with an irony that King Solomon, now fallen from his wisdom, can no longer perceive:

> But king Solomon loved many strange women, together with the daughter of Pharaoh, women of Moabites, Amonites, Edomites, Zidonians, and Hittites; of the nations concerning which the Lord said unto the children of Israel, Ye shall not go into them [see Deuteronomy 23:3]. . . . For Solomon went after Ashtoreth the goddess of the Zidonians and after Milcom the abomination of the Ammonites. And Solomon did evil in the sight of the Lord.

The narrator of King Solomon's life shapes the arc of his story so that it reaches its zenith and then turns downward, like a failed rocket. At the end of Solomon's trajectory, his purpose is not to enhance monotheistic wisdom but to amass palaces of gold, to acquire chariots and navies, to possess concubines galore, and to marshal battalions of foreign wives, each of whom is accompanied by a foreign god. No longer able to work with ideas, he covets power; and, without the capacity to understand the meaning of value, he values navies and gold.

The indictment against him in I Kings 9 begins with his quest for military allies and armaments:

> And king Solomon made a navy of ships in Ezion-Geber, which is besides Eloth, on the shore of the Red Sea, in the land of Edom. And Hiram [King of Tyre] sent in the navy his servants, shipmen that had knowledge of the sea, with the servants of Solomon. And they came to Ophir, and they fetched from thence gold, four hundred and twenty talents, and brought it to king Solomon.

Now at this time, Solomon had just finished two great houses, one for the worship of God, known now as the First Temple, and the other for himself, the showplace for his opulence. This emphasis on double houses suggests Solomon's loyalties are ambivalent. And it is the house of opulence that most impresses the Queen of Sheba when she visits.

Though she also notes the grandeur of the Temple, the Queen's intimacy with Solomon is entirely based on their sharing the dictates of the sex goddess, Ashtoreth, and on their love of gold and the other valuable gifts that they exchange, as we see in I Kings 10. First the lovely Queen sweet talks the impressionable King about being blessed by the Lord, and then she briskly moves on to gold, spices, and sex:

> Blessed be the Lord thy God, which delighted in thee, to set thee on the throne of Israel: because the Lord loved Israel for ever, therefore made he thee king, to do judgment and justice. And she gave the king a hundred and twenty talents of gold, and of spices great store, and precious stones: there came no more such abundance of spices as these which the Queen of Sheba gave to King Solomon. . . . And king Solomon gave unto the Queen of Sheba all her desire, whatsoever she asked, besides that which Solomon gave her of his royal bounty. So she turned and went to her own country, she and her servants.

After her pricey fling with King Solomon, the Queen goes home, "all her desire" satisfied, which, in the realm of "all," included sexual fulfillment, "besides that which Solomon gave her of his royal bounty."

In the *Tanach*, turning back from the Children of Israel to one's own country is shorthand for turning away from monotheism to idolatry, as in the case of Jethro. He, after serving as a valued advisor of Moses, refuses Moses' generous offer to join the Hebrews. So, in Exodus 18:27, "Moses let his father-in-law depart; and he went his way to his own land." Even an intelligent man like Jethro could not grasp the full intelligence of monotheism, and neither could the captivating Queen of Sheba; both go home to their own land, to their own way of thinking, and their own desires.

At the end of his life, Solomon did remain in Jerusalem, in that he was "buried in the city of David his father," but the man who was buried was not the man we like to remember, as we see in I Kings 11:4-8:

> For it came to pass, when Solomon was old, that his wives turned away his heart: and his heart was not perfect with the Lord his God, as was the heart of David his father. . . . And Solomon did evil in the sight of the Lord, and went not fully with the Lord, as did David his father. . . . Then did Solomon build on high places for Chemosh, the abomination of Moab, in the hill before Jerusalem, and for Molech, the abomination of the children of Ammon. And likewise did he for all his strange wives which burnt incense and sacrificed unto their gods.

The repetitive assertions that Solomon's "heart was not perfect with the Lord his God, as was David his father," and "Solomon . . . went not fully with the Lord, as did David his father," are doubly ambiguous in both English and Hebrew. Was David like his son in that he went not fully with the Lord, or was he unlike his son in that he never, despite his other sins, set up sites for idolatrous worship, as did Solomon? Were both father and son faulty in their wisdom? Or was it just Solomon?

The ancient rabbis, already unhappy to accept that the wise Solomon "did evil in the sight of the Lord," needed to avoid the possibility that David was as sinful as Solomon, even though he clearly was. Given what we know about what David did most of his life, and what the elderly Solomon did at the end of his life, it is likely that we are meant to understand that Solomon resembled his father in ways that the *Tanach* urges its readers to condemn. Both David and Solomon did enough evil in the sight of the Lord to remind the Children of Israel how easy it is to abandon reason and follow the whimsical gods that are worshipped on high places. Like King David, King Solomon lives today as an ideal Jew. But he is also a reminder of an unfortunate truth: the capacity to think wisely is fragile.

Because Solomon's wisdom was particularly fragile, the nation he led could not last long, and indeed it did not. The last story we have of the wise King's reign concerns his mismanagement of the House of Israel to the point that it was soon divided. Under his successor, Jeroboam, ten of the twelve tribes seceded, as we learn in this carefully-crafted passage in I Kings11:28-38:

> And the man Jeroboam was a mighty man of valor: and Solomon seeing the young man that he was industrious, he made him ruler over all the charge of the house of Joseph [i.e., of the two tribes of Ephraim and Menasseh, named after Joseph's two sons]. And it came to pass that when Jeroboam went out of Jerusalem, that the prophet Ahijah . . .

found him in the way; and he had clad himself with a new garment; and they two were alone in the field: And Ahijah caught [took hold of] the new garment that was on him, and rent it in twelve pieces: And he said to Jeroboam, Take these ten pieces [representing Ephraim and Menasseh and the other eight tribes that make up the "ten lost tribes"] for thus saith the Lord, the God of Israel, Behold, I will rend the kingdom out of the hand of Solomon, and will give ten to thee. . . . Because they have forsaken me, and have worshipped Ashtoreth the goddess of the Zidonians, Chemosh the god of the Moabites, and Milcom the god of the children of Ammon . . . . and have not walked in my ways, to do that which is right in mine eyes and to keep my statutes and my judgments, as did David his father. Howbeit, I will not take the whole kingdom out of his hand: but will make him prince [over the diminished territory of Judah and Benjamin] all the days of his life. . . . And it shall be, if thou [Jeroboam] will hearken unto all that I shall command thee . . . . as did David my servant did: that I will be with thee, and build thee a secure house, as I built for David, and will give Israel unto thee.

There are several problems here that have plagued interpreters for two millennia. The first is the claim that David, as a perfect exemplar of following God's commandments, deserved a "secure house." This patently contradicts the ancient rabbis' belief that God kept David from building the First Temple because of his less-than-righteous history.

A second issue is Wise King Solomon's demotion to serve as "prince" of a rump nation. Is not this punishment more severe than what we might reasonably expect for this wisest of men?

And thirdly, might we not expect this famously wise king to find a wise way of dealing with his being replaced by Jeroboam, a man whom he himself deemed "a mighty man of valor"? But Solomon does not choose wisely. In I Kings 40, we learn what the King did after learning about his demotion:

> Solomon sought therefore to kill Jeroboam. And Jeroboam arose, and fled into Egypt, unto Shishak king of Egypt, and was in Egypt until the death of Solomon.

There is a bit of Cain in Solomon, for he too has murder woven into his wise creativity. And, is there not an allusion to Cain's meeting of Abel "in the field" in the passage above describing the meeting of Ahijah and Jeroboam when "they two were alone in the field"?

The rabbinic tradition of interpretation, called *midrash*, draws on just this linking of parallel stories via allusion. In any case, Solomon, here at the end of his career, is indeed both wise and murderous, and that is probably why his punishment is so severe. This corruption of Hebraic wisdom simply could not be tolerated.

Jeroboam outwits Solomon by fleeing to Egypt, even though the Hebrews had been commanded on multiple occasions never to return there, as in Deuteronomy 17:15-16:

> Thou mayest not set a stranger over thee, which is not thy brother. . . . He shall not . . . cause the people to return to Egypt . . . . Ye shall henceforth return no more that way.

But Solomon left Jeroboam no other choice than to seek refuge under King Shishak in Egypt. As could be expected from the Hebrews previous experience in Egypt, serving Shishak was not a happy experience. Shishak, a warrior king, who later conquered Judah and sacked Jerusalem with 60,000 horseman and carried off much booty, including "all the shields of gold which Solomon made," as we learn in I Kings 14:25-26. This looting of his coveted treasure does not reflect well on the legacy of Solomon the Wise.

Whether King David was wiser than his son, or the other way around, or both were less wise than they should have been, is less important than a clear understanding of Hebraic wisdom, which rests on adherence to a single, invisible God's vision of a just society, free of idolatrous nonsense at all times and all seasons.

To this day, Jews remain oblivious to the denouement of Solomon's story. But Christian theologians and European artists were eager to memorialize this Hebrew King's diminishment, as we see in this Seventeenth-century

painting, "*Samson Worships Idols*," by Marcantonio Frances-
chini. Under the supervision of the lissome Queen of Sheba
and a few of his concubines, the humble King kneels to a
marble statue, to a bizarre fusion of a fertility goddess and
the Virgin Mary. The painting's startling message in the
Seventeenth century, which was meant for European Christians, was the same as the *Tanach*'s message for the ancient
Hebrews; they were not as wise as they were supposed to be:

CHAPTER NINE
Literalism and its Humor

I: Naaman's Folly

Idolaters are literalists. They prostrate themselves to things, to stones, stars, bulls, and sex-goddesses carved from burnt logs. The ancient Hebrews, when they weren't aligning themselves with the minions of Ashtoreth, tried their faltering best to hold in their minds the abstract commandments of their abstract Lord. So strong was the Hebrews temptation to return to literal thinking, that the *Tanach* contains a story in II Kings 5 that appears to have no other purpose than to mock the literalist mind of Naaman, the Captain of Syria's Army:

> Now Naaman, captain of the host of the king of Syria, was a great man with his master, and honourable, because by him the Lord had given deliverance

unto Syria: he was also a mighty man of valour, but he was a leper. And the Syrians had gone out by companies, and had brought away a captive out of the land of Israel a little maid; and she waited on Naaman's wife. And she said unto her mistress, Would God my lord was with the prophet that is in Samaria! For he would recover him from his leprosy. And one went in, and told his lord [what the little maid said] . . . And the king of Syria said, . . . Go, and I will send a letter unto the king of Israel. And he [Naaman] departed, and took with him ten talents of silver, and six thousand pieces of gold, and ten changes of raiment. And he brought the letter to the king of Israel, saying, Now when this letter is come unto thee, behold, I have sent Naaman my servant to thee, that thou mayest recover him of his leprosy.

This artful narrative sets up a contrast between the "little maid," who understands that a Hebrew prophet is needed to cure leprosy, and Naaman, who thinks that what is needed is silver, gold, and fancy clothes to impress the King of Israel. And the gap between literal wealth and a wealth of spiritual understanding gets wider:

And it came to pass when the king of Israel [Jehoram] had read the letter, that he rent his clothes, and said, Am I God, to kill and to make alive, that this man [the King of Syria] doth send unto me to recover a man [Naaman] of his leprosy [a disease not treatable until the Twentieth century]? Wherefore consider, I pray you, and see how he seeketh a quarrel against me.

Jehoram, too, does not understand what is going on. Because he knows that the literal disease of leprosy is incurable, he assumes that the king of Syria is trying to pick a fight with him so that he can invade yet again on the pretext that Israel has refused his reasonable request. Matters look ominous; leprosy is not curable and Syria will soon invade.

But when Elisha, "the man of God," hears about this dangerous state of affairs, he actually cures Naaman, not by a medical treatment but by moving the story into a metaphorical realm.

In a moment we will address the question of what exactly the *Tanach* means by leprosy, but first let us observe how Naaman maintains his literalist view as Elisha's treatment comes to a successful conclusion:

> So Naaman came with his horses and chariot, and stood at the door of the house of Elisha. And Elisha sent a messenger unto him, saying, Go and wash in Jordan seven times, and thy flesh shall come again to thee, and thou shall be clean. But Naaman was wroth, and went away, and said, Behold, I thought he will surely come out to me, and stand and call on the name of the Lord his God and strike his hand over the [affected] place, and recover the leper. Are not . . . the rivers of Damascus better than all the waters of Israel? May I not wash in them and be clean? So he went away in a rage.

And his servants came near . . and said, My father,
if the prophet had bid thee do some great thing,
wouldst thou not have done it? How much [easier
it would be to obey] when he saith to thee, Wash
and be clean. Then went he down, and dipped himself seven times in Jordan, according to the man of
God: and his flesh came again like unto the flesh of
a little child, and he was clean.

His cure of course impresses Naaman, so he quickly returns to Elisha to proclaim a change of heart, at least
somewhat so:

Behold, now I know there is no God in all the
earth, but in Israel: now therefore, I pray thee, take
a blessing [i.e., money] of thy servant. But he [Eli-
sha] said, As the Lord liveth, before whom I stand,
I will receive none. And he [Naaman] begged him
[Elisha] to accept it; but he refused.

Unable to understand that he is speaking to a man who
works in an ethereal mode, for which he takes no money,
Naaman politely pushes himself deeper into his concrete
hole:

And Naanan said, Shall there not then, I pray
thee, be given to thy servant two mules' burden of
earth? For thy servant will offer henceforth neither
burnt offering nor sacrifice unto other gods, but
unto the Lord [sacrifices for which his imported
Hebrew mud will be put to good service].

When Naaman says that he now realizes that there is "no God in all the earth but in Israel," it turns out that he means this literally, and, in a comic moment, he proceeds to haul a "two mules' burden of earth" back to Syria, where he will perform pagan rites for the God of Israel.

In case we miss this mockery of literalist thinking, the story goes on to distinguish the abstract values of Elisha, a true man of God, with the literalist values of Elisha's servant, Gehazi, who is most interested in filthy lucre. He chases after Naaman and catches him to take advantage of the rich man's gold and silver. And Naaman does shed money on Gehazi, which leads Elisha to punish Gehazi with poetic justice:

> The leprosy therefore of Naaman shall cleave unto thee, and unto thy seed forever. And he [Gehazi] went out from his presence a leper as white as snow.

Let us now be clear about the meaning of *leprosy* in the *Tanach*. This emblematic affliction could indeed affect skin, but also clothes, walls, stones, and even entire households. Much to the surprise of many readers of this story, leprosy is *not* the skin disease described by the Norwegian physician, Gerhard Armauer Hansen, in 1873, nor any fleshly disease at all. It is an extended metaphor for a wide range of unholy deficiencies deep in the Hebrew mind, represented by discolorations of skin, or clothes, or stone foundations, for which no doctor is needed. Rather a priest inspects the depth, color, and seriousness of these symbolic blotches and then prescribes not salves but appropriate atonement on the Temple Mount, as outlined in Leviticus 13 and 14. Leprosy is thus not a literal disease but an indication that Hebraic sanctity has been violated, an idea about which the literalist Naaman, and his Hebrew sympathizers, could have no understanding.

CHAPTER TEN
EXTREME DESIRE, OR COVETING

I: NARCISSUS

From their reading of Homer's and Ovid's careful observation of human behavior, the ancient Greeks knew that emotion often became overwhelmingly intense, as in the case of Achilles' wrath and Paris' passion for Helen of Troy. But without a science of psychology, the inquisitive Greeks, as usual, attributed over-active passion to mischievous gods.

Ovid tells us the story of Narcissus, who at birth was so lovely that his mother found it necessary to consult Tiresias, the prophet of Apollo, about what to do with this beautiful boy. The blind seer predicted that the boy would live a long life only if he never discovered himself. This warning against self-understanding was not an attack on psychotherapy, which did not then exist, but a recognition that self-exploration would inevitably lead to an encounter with the unpredictable gods who were in charge of everyone's fate, often fatally so, as in the case of Oedipus.

Though Narcissus indeed grows up to be exquisitely handsome, he unexpectedly shows no interest in romance, and thus he neglects the local mountain nymphs who yearn for his attention. Narcissus's rejection of the eager nymphs enrages Aphrodite, who sends her emissary, Nemesis, the goddess of Revenge, to arrange appropriate punishment. Thus, on seeing his own beautiful face in a pool of water, Narcissus freezes in a state of perpetual self-adoration, burning internally from the blaze of his passion, until the gods mercifully transmogrified him into the golden flower we know today.

This myth highlights many intense feelings, extreme self-love, the deep disappointment of frustrated nymphs, the outrageous revenge of angry goddesses, the asinine mercy of their forgiveness, and the hyper-absurd metamorphosis of Narcissus. But none of this is formally linked to any aspect of the human mind, for the poet Ovid was not a psychologist, of which there were none in his day.

We no longer look to gods or poets for psychological explanations, consulting trained psychiatrists instead. In 1899, Paul Näcke located narcissism in the brain as a sexual perversion. Freud, as usual, tried his best to contribute something new to this conversation. In his essay of 1914, "On Narcissism: an Introduction," Freud, still without the ability to correlate his ideas with brain anatomy, discussed the problem of intense self-love in terms of his abstract "pleasure principle," wherever that might be in the brain, and concluded, without evidence, that narcissism is a disguise for repressed homosexuality.

The localization of an actual pleasure center in the human brain did not occur until James Olds and Peter Milner at McGill University demonstrated that electrical stimulation in the right place in the brains of rats would intensify their sensation of pleasure. With electrodes placed in the nucleus accumbens, just superior to the olfactory bulb (where perfumes and pheromones are registered in dogs and man), the rats would continually push a lever that provided hits of cocaine, which in turn produced a surcharge of fatal dopamine. The rats continued demanding hyper-pleasurable cocaine until they died of starvation, for they had stopped pushing the lever for food.

Similarly, studies of human addicts have demonstrated that the nucleus accumbens is where nicotine, opium, alcohol, and other addictive substances produce their sticky pleasures, which often do become so intense that they lead to death. This opened a scientific way to explore excessive states of mind. Interestingly, in his five essays on energy-giving cocaine, Freud denied that cocaine was addictive.

But Freud did note that the brain possessed a mechanism for bringing into the foreground a selected person, object, or feeling. He coined a name for this mechanism, *libidobesetzung* (changed in the English translation of his work to *cathexis,* a Greek-derived word). Cathexis is the process by which the mind focuses its attention on the object of its most important desire at the moment. This was not a process of intensifying a desire but of selecting an object that would satisfy the urgent desire in question.

That the brain also has a separate capacity to intensify what it has brought to the foreground escaped the celebrated Freud. For according to this innovative psychoanalyst, whatever chaotic memories a troubled young brain happened to retain from childhood are sufficient in themselves to explain the neuroses that that Freud claimed to have found in his patients' minds. Freud's neuroses are not intensifications of normal aspects of the mind but static manifestations of what has long been simmering in the id's roiling memory. The goal of psychoanalytic therapy, says Freud, is to move these memories into the ego, where they can be better managed.

It appears so unlikely that we might find any important contribution to our modern understanding of pathologically intense passion in the Hebrew Bible that hardly anybody bothers looking for it there. But there it is, hiding in plain sight.

Let us begin by distinguishing delusional thinking, which we have already discussed, from an intensification of normal thinking. One can apparently sacrifice ones child to the god Moloch with a calm belief that this delusional act honors a protective god. And one can act like Moses, who, with intense, irrational passion, smashes God's inscribed tablets as a way of delivering a justified rebuke to the children of Israel's crazed forging of the golden calf, their new god who freed them from Egypt.

We observe that a human being can be calmly irrational, or can make rational sense while being emotionally overwrought, or, on occasion, be calmly rational. Intensity is not a measure of truth or error. It is its own psychological force, often the driver of dangerous proclivities, and just as often a driver of righteous insistence on justice.

The mind's capacity to act with pathologic intensity is the subject of the last of the Ten Commandments, as given in Exodus 20:17-20:

> Thou shalt not covet thy neighbor's house, thou shalt not covet thy neighbor's wife, nor his manservant, nor his ox, nor his ass, nor anything that is thy neighbor's. And all the people saw the thunderings, and the lightnings, and the noise of the trumpet, and the mountain smoking: and when the people saw it, they removed and stood afar off. And they said unto Moses, Speak thou with us, and we will hear; but let not God speak with us, lest we die. And Moses said unto the people, Fear not: for God has come to prove [test] you, and let his fear [i.e., "your awe for Him] be before your faces, that you sin not.

The multiplicity of opportunities for the Children of Israel to covet one thing or another is so alarming that the Tenth Commandment is heralded with "thunderings" and "lightenings."

But the meaning of the Tenth Commandment has remained puzzling during the entire three millennia of its existence. Hebrew scholars have not even been able to agree on why the commandment exists at all, other than God thought it so important that He legislated it from the top of Mount Sinai at a time when the hungry children of Israel were not coveting much beyond food and water in the parching desert.

The Twelfth-century commentator on the *Tanach*, Abraham Ibn Ezra, faced the problem squarely. Here is Kaeren Fish's translation of Ibn Ezra's writing on the Tenth Commandment:

> Many people are amazed at this command-ment. They ask, how is it possible for a person **not** to covet in his heart [mind] all beautiful things that appear desirable to him.

Ibn Ezra realized that an intense desire for somebody else's property is a psychological perversion that requires a psychological explanation, but he lacked sufficient psycho-logical training to make a convincing analysis. He resorted to a parable whose proposed interpretation does not capture how human minds actually work:

> Now I shall present a parable: Know that a peasant who is of sound mind, and who sees a prin-cess who is beautiful, will not covet in his heart to lie with her, for he knows that it is impossible . . . . Likewise, a person does not desire to lie with his

mother, although she may be beautiful, for he has been accustomed since his youth to know that she is forbidden to him. In the same way, . . . [when] an intelligent person . . . knows that God has forbidden his neighbor's wife to him, that she is more elevated in his eyes than the princess in the eyes of the peasant. And so he is satisfied with his portion and does not allow his heart to covet and desire something that is not his, for he knows that God does not wish to give it to him.

Ibn Ezra's analogy within his pseudo-parable is misconceived, and his understanding of psychology is non-existent, despite setting his argument in a psychological frame. Parables recited by an intelligent man like the prophet Nathan to the intelligent King David should call to mind a truth that is not immediately obvious but soon becomes so. David, for instance, after a brief delay and a little prodding, recognizes himself as the miscreant in Nathan's parable.

Ibn Ezra's parable has no such power, for this otherwise-intelligent commentator does not in this instance have a coherent message to bring to light. It is not true that a man of low social status will refrain from fantasizing about a delectable princess simply because she is unavailable, just as a married man will not refrain from lusting after a pin-up of his favorite Hollywood actress just because the lady would ignore him.

And a Jew who is told in the First Commandment to worship no idol, and in the Tenth Commandment not to covet his neighbor's wife, will disobey both without regard for the fact that the commandments had been legislated by God from the heights of Mount Sinai. Contrary to Ibn Ezra, comparative social status does not affect desire.

Obadia ben Jacob Sforno, the early Sixteenth-century, Italian physician and commentator on the *Tanach*, could not, like Ibn Ezra, understand why the transient coveting of everything from a neighbor's oxen to his wife could by itself be of sufficient importance to earn a place in the Ten Commandments. Therefore, says Rabbi Sforno, one must prohibit coveting to keep it from progressing to something worse: "Once you begin to covet something belonging to someone else it is only a short step to committing robbery."

This view is seconded in modern times by Dennis Prager, the intelligent and popular radio host, in his short book, *The Ten Commandments*: "Coveting is what leads to violating the preceding four commandments—the ones against murder, adultery, stealing, and perjury." Prager understands that the Biblical term for "covet" does not refer to mere envy or mere lust; what the term prohibits, in Prager's view, is the intensification of normal human inclinations to an evil end. "And that is what the Tenth Commandment Prohibits."

And this is probably correct. But Prager does not name or localize the force that drives normal desire to an evil end, nor does he explain why the commandments against murder, adultery, stealing, and perjury are not sufficient in themselves. But he does realize that if the mere desire for a lakefront mansion were a sin, atonement would never end and would accomplish nothing.

But what if we are dealing with an independent capacity of the human brain that might let sleeping dogs lie, or turn them loose in a rabid rage? What if desire is not a problem until a separate force intensifies it into a state beyond control?

One can be a murderer, and one can be a sadistic, serial murderer; one can be moderately kind or intensely kind, like Mother Theresa. One can be extreme in anything. What the Tenth Commandment attempts to moderate is the unpredictable human capacity to intensify and thereby corrupt any feeling, and any plan of action.

The *Tanach* implies that the mind's capacity to intensify is independent of the thoughts and feelings that it might intensify. One can intensify "justice" until one has murdered a hundred million people with Stalin's and Mao's communism. The Tenth Commandment is in the same vein as Aristotle's warning to avoid extremes and seek a moderate temper, the *via media*.

This Hebraic view distinguishes itself from the prevalent view of ancient physicians, who in general did not seriously follow Aristotle's *via media*. For centuries the followers of the Hippocratic corpus conceived of the mind as animated by four distinct humors, whose mixture varied from one person to another, thus producing different character types. In general, this mixture of humors resulted in four basic personalities. People born with a predominance of the humor blood inevitably became sanguine, with the humor phlegm phlegmatic, with black bile melancholic, and those dominated by yellow bile lived with enormous passion, easy to seduce and easy to anger.

For this last type of angry, libidinous character there was no room for further intensification, for no further stimulus would be needed to precipitate the Trojan War and all its miseries. And the behavior of the other three could not be intensified, for their personalities were fixed from the time of their creation.

Because this Hippocratic view did not fade away until the Nineteenth century, Shakespeare, in his *Julius Caesar* of 1599, could draw on Hippocratic understanding when he had Mark Antony eulogize Brutus in terms of the four humors (or "elements"):

> This was the noblest Roman of them all. All the rest of the conspirators acted out of jealousy of great Caesar. Only he acted from honesty and for the general good. His life was gentle, and the elements mixed so well in him that Nature might stand up and say to all the world, 'This was a man.'

But Shakespeare obviously knew that Brutus' life was not entirely "gentle," nor did Brutus act entirely "from honesty and the general good." He was much in doubt about his decision to join the conspirators, and afterwards he was tormented by dreams of the ghost of Caesar. Caesar himself is surprised by Brutus's unexpected regicidal violence; he howls his famous last words, "*Et tu, Bruté*," a Latin phrase which Shakespeare's English audience would hear as, "And you, too, Brute?" If a mixture of Hippocratic humors did not fully determine Brutus' behavior, what did drive him to become a brute? Why did he not remain gentle?

Not even Shakespeare fully understood the powerful agency that could drive hesitating Brutus to join the conspirators. Nor did the conspirators themselves recognize the agency that alchemized their jealous resentment into murder. On their way to the Senate to assassinate the Emperor, they paused to quarrel about where the sun would rise that morning, pointing their swords in competing directions, demonstrating that their intense, free-floating zeal knew not where it was leading them.

The ancient Hebrews may have been the first to realize that the mind did in fact contain an agency that could hyper-inflate any belief and any action. Many years later the fields of psychology and literature gave us the tools to understand how intensification of human feeling is managed by what Tennessee Williams called, in a metaphoric sense, "a streetcar named desire," the motor that can drive human desire of every kind into tragedy.

Vernacular language often borrows from the Tenth Commandment to warn about the mind's tendency to make mountains out of molehills, to fall crazy in love, to hitch our wagon to a distant star, and to tell a loved-one to drop dead. We think we say what we mean, but what we mean is on a streetcar driven we know not where by an anonymous, impromptu conductor. We exaggerate and minimize, utter lame excuses, overpromise and underprepare, make a mess of everything, procrastinate or go off half cocked, all the while ignoring the urgent need to regulate our brain's conductor, wherever it is stationed in the brain. We should not let our minds go overboard about anything, but we do, sometimes blaming the devil.

Knowing the meaning of the Hebrew phrase for "Do not covet," *Lo Tachmood*, might guide us to a better understanding of the Tenth commandment's warning against hyper-enthusiasm. The root of this verb in modern Hebrew signifies an intense but appropriate love for children, other family members, and close friends, whom we call *chamudi*, "my dear one." But In the *Tanach*, this root not only connotes an appropriately intense love, but also an intensification of hate, and an inappropriately intense rejection of what should be desired, as in Proverbs 21:20:

> There is treasure to be desired (*nechmad*), an oil in the dwelling of the wise; but a foolish man spendeth [spitteth] it up.

In the *Tanach* the "foolish man" is usually not the idolater, for he has no choice, but the Children of Israel, who do. Thus, in Psalm 106:24-25, David has nothing but contempt for the contemptuous children of Israel, who despised the Land they are meant to cherish:

Yea, they despised the pleasant [*chemda*] land, they believed not his word: But murmured in their tents, and hearkened not unto the voice of the Lord. Therefore he lifted up his hand against them, to overthrow them in the wilderness.

There is a multiplicity of intense negativity here, murmuring, despising, disobedience, wilderness, and reciprocal overthrowing; the Children of Israel overthrow God, and He overthrows them for their failure to recognize the sanctity of the Land they have been given. This intensity frequently lifts its roaring head and becomes, in the *Tanach*, a central feature of human behavior, both for good and for evil, as in the case of David.

One particularly moving use of the root of the Hebrew word for coveting [CHMD] is in the first chapter of the Book of Lamentations, where the exiled Hebrews in Babylon mourn their lost city of Jerusalem:

The adversary hath spread out his hand upon all her pleasant things [*machmedah*]: for she hath seen that the heathen entered into her sanctuary, whom thou didst command that they would not enter into thy congregation.

The sadness of loss is deepened into despair when the mind's engine of intensification turns up its volume, which was appropriate for mourning the disastrous loss of Jerusalem, but on other occasions not.

Let us then go back to Ibn Ezra's starting point, for he correctly noted that the Tenth Commandment requires psychological clarification. The Hebrew mind is prone, like all minds, to push itself into hyper-intense states, the result of which we now call megalomania, a psychiatric diagnosis whose name has now been changed in the Diagnostic and Statistical Manual of Mental Disorders to various forms of the Narcissistic Personality Disorder, based on Ovid's portrayal of Narcissus' extreme pre-occupation with himself. What is central to all Narcissistic Personality disorders is not the objects of intense feeling, which vary, but the mental capacity for intensification itself.

Paris' desire to bed the gorgeous Helen while a guest in her husband's home would not concern the Torah, because in itself it is not a mortal danger to rational living. But when he actually stole her away, his lust became a major problem, fueled by his pre-existing, inflammable, and uncontrollable capacity for intensification.

The character of Korach seems to have no other function in the *Tanach* than to illustrate the mind's capacity for intensification, independent of any particular idea one might exaggerate. Korach is just the kind of man who is susceptible to getting overheated. A charismatic mesmerizer, an electrifying motivator, a rebel without a cause, he is full of hot air, a hollow man.

The Tenth Commandment does not forbid normal desire; it forbids megalomaniac firebrands and their destructive loss of self-control. Korach, an esteemed member of the

Levites, the cousin of Moses, is nevertheless dissatisfied with his status; he is absolutely convinced that he would be a better administrator of God's rational laws than Moses himself. And then he arouses a mob to overthrow the impostor. He is pathologic intensity personified.

II: Korach: Excessive Pursuit of Power

Korach's full story is told in Numbers 16, but let us begin with David's summary of Korach's exploits in Psalm 106:7-18. The Poet-King, speaking directly to God, sets Korach's attempt to wrest power from Moses in the context of the Hebrews' persistent ingratitude. From the time their God led them safely across the Red Sea, the Children of Israel repetitively complained, indeed like children. Were there not sufficient graves in Egypt to save them from dying of thirst or starvation in the desert? Was not Egypt a fertile land, with food aplenty? Would they not improve their lot by returning to their brick-laying jobs in Egypt immediately?

The Israelites' disgruntled complaining elides smoothly into David's story of Korach. But the psalmist will not honor the hopeful usurper by mentioning his name, perhaps because David recognizes himself in the rebel's intense impudence:

> Our fathers understood not thy wonders in Egypt; they remembered not the multitude of thy mercies; but they provoked Him at the sea, even

at the Red sea. . . . And He saved them from the hand of him [Pharaoh] that hated them, and redeemed them from the hand of the enemy. . . . They soon forgot his works; they waited not for his counsel, but lusted exceedingly in the wilderness, and tempted God in the desert. They [Korach and his gang of high-placed rebels] envied Moses also in the camp, and Aaron the saint of the Lord.

In King David's mind, Korach was distinguishable from other stiff-necked Hebrews only by his intensity. As the leader of a large cabal, he enacted a more strident form of rebellion. He craved power for power's sake, without the slightest idea about how to use it. Presumably, his recruits were also empty-headed men with immense, vacuous energy.

Let us turn to Numbers 16:1 for more details about Korach's rebellion and his consequent cruel and unusual punishment, apparently chosen to match the intense nature of his crime:

Now Korah, the son of Izahar, the son of Kohat, the son of Levi, and Dathan an Abiram, the sons of Eliab, and On, the some of Pleth, sons of Reuven, took *men*:

The King-James translator chose to add to this verse the noun "*men*," placed in italics, because the original Hebrew contains no direct object for the verb "took," thus giving the impression that Korach took nothing into his rebellion but his inflated aspirations. He would march forward, along with his comrades, especially Dathan and Abiram, with no armament beyond his fancy pedigree. Numbers 16 continues his story:

> And they rose up before Moses, . . . two hundred and fifty princes of the assembly, famous in the congregation, men of renown: And they gathered themselves together against Moses and against Aaron, and they said to them, Ye take too much upon you, seeing all the congregation are holy, every one of them, and the Lord is among them: wherefore then lift ye up above the congregation of the Lord? And when Moses heard it, he fell upon his face:

Moses, a modest man who at the onset of his leadership of the enslaved Hebrews told God that he was tongue-tied and unfit, finally agreeing to lead only when God promised the assistance of Aaron, who would serve as his spokesman. Now, on being confronted by Korach, Moses again shows his character by falling with humility "upon his face," placing himself in vivid contrast to the blow-hard Korach and his supporters, Dathan and Abiram. The true leader is gentle, but these three passionate adversaries claim that Egypt is the true land of milk and honey, and the land of Canaan a fraud:

> And Moses said unto Korah, Hear, I pray you, ye sons of Levi: Seemeth it but a small thing unto you, that the God of Israel hath separated you from

the congregation of Israel, to bring you near to himself to do the service of the tabernacle of the Lord, and to stand before the congregation to minister unto them? . . . . And Moses sent to call Dathan and Abiram, the sons of Eliab, who said, . . . Is it a small thing that thou [Moses] hath brought us up out of a land [Egypt] that floweth with milk and honey, to kill us in the wilderness except [so that] thou make thyself altogether a prince over us? Moreover thou hast not brought us to a land that floweth with milk and honey, or given us inheritance of fields and vineyards. Wilt thou put out the eyes of these men? . . . . And Moses was very wroth, and said unto the Lord, . . . I have not taken one ass from them, neither have I hurt one of them.

What Dathan and Abiram mean by their last question (Wilt thou put out the eyes of these men?) is an indignant pronouncement that they are fully aware that their phony leader is deceiving them.

Of course we are meant to see that it is the conspirators who suffer from misperception and misunderstanding, driven by a force that is so strong that it distorts their sense of reality. And perhaps we can see that Moses responds to the mischievous conspirators with an allusion to the Tenth Commandment: he has not coveted a single ass belonging to them, nor has he resorted to violence to obtain what he desires. He has not "hurt one of them," he says, perhaps recalling the time in his youth when he, with an hyper-inflated anger, killed an Egyptian who was beating a Hebrew slave, an impulsive crime for which he was banished to Midian.

To repel Korach's perverse attack against Moses requires an even stronger counter-force. The divinely staged punishment of Korach and his associates is, again, not a miracle, nor is it meant to be an appropriate legal sentence. Its bizarre intensity is rather a measure of the mind's unruly capacity for going overboard, as well as a measure of the power needed to control an unacceptable display of megalomania:

> And Moses said, . . . if the Lord make a new thing, and the earth open her mouth, and swallow them up, with all that appertain unto them, and they go down quick into the pit; then ye shall understand that these men have provoked the Lord. And it came to pass, as he had made an end of speaking all these words that the ground clave asunder that was under them: And the earth opened her mouth and swallowed them up, and their houses, and all the men that appertained unto Korah, and all their goods. They and all that appertained to them, went down alive into the pit, and the earth closed upon them: and they perished from among the congregation.

The parsimonious style of the *Tanach* usually avoids wasting words, but the repetitive description of the earth breaking asunder and opening her mouth serves a purpose here. The overly-intensified description of Korach's demise matches Korach's overblown zeal. Korach's way of dying also matches the fate of those who prayed to the Golden Calf; both groups were cut off from "among the congregation" because of their misplaced and uncontrolled zealotry. On both occasions multitudes died for immense abominations. The mind's capacity for immensity requires a great act of dampening.

The ancient rabbis were so unnerved by the intensity of the "new thing" used for Korach's punishment that they devised, in the Talmudic Tractate, *Pirkei Avoth*, a myth about God's having created at the last minute of the sixth day of creation ten special tools to be held in reserve. One of these was a sinkhole specifically designed to gulp down the living Korach, including his household, all his followers, their entire families, their houses and their livestock, everything that could possibly be coveted by hyperactive coveters, an intense punishment for an intense crime.

III: Zealous Punishment for Zealous Idolatry

The power of misplaced zealotry plagued the minds of thoughtful Israelites from the beginning. No matter how often they were reprimanded, they could not discard their powerful infatuation with idolatry. This, too, demanded an intense counter-force, as we see in the story of Phinehas' double slaying of a "man of Israel," named Zimri, and his "Midianitish woman," named Cozbi, as told in Numbers 25:

And Israel joined himself to Ba-al Peor [the lord of the House of Horus]: and the anger of the Lord was kindled against Israel. . . . And, behold, one of the children of Israel came and brought unto his brethren a Midianitish woman in the sight of Moses, and in the sight of all the congregation. . . . And when Phinehas, the son of Eleazar, the son of Aaron the priest, saw it, he rose up from among the congregation, and took a javelin in his hand; And he went after the man of Israel unto the tent, and thrust both of them through, the man of Israel, and the woman through her belly.

This pornographic story of a priest skewering two fornicators was not intended to titillate, but to focus attention on the persistent difficulties that the Hebrews encountered in cooling their appetite for strange women and their foreign gods.

Notice how a single anatomic detail, "belly," forces the reader to visualize the exact physical positions of the lovers and the javelin-wielding Phinehas. Given the Torah's sacred foundation, the message of this story must be of a more elevated nature than that of mere pornography. Zimri's overheated sex with an idolatress could be mastered only by an equally-intense counterattack, as captured by the Sixteenth-century Flemish artist, Joos van Winghe:

This composition of salaciously jangled limbs, ominous black patches, and glaring primary colors is echoed by the equally threatening weather just outside the opening of Zimri's tent. Both the biblical text and Winghe's painting portray just how much creative energy must be expended to control the intensity of idolatrous passion.

Like all good paintings, this one by Winghe is not a mere representation of an event but a carefully-composed visualization of the *idea* behind the event. In my view, both the ability to read and understand a literary story, and the ability to interpret a well-endowed painting, derive from the same mental capacity. One perceives not only the skill by which the story or the painting is rendered, and not only how the artful composition contributes to the effect of the whole, but also, and most importantly, how all of the relevant details of the work are integrated into an *idea* that is important enough to compel our attention.

Both Winghe's painting and the biblical story of the slaying of Zimri and Cozbi artfully contrast two opposing views of life, one as riotous as stormy weather and idolatrous sex, and the other as harmonious as ethical monotheism, whose desecration must be countered by a matching intensity. In the upper right corner, two of the jangled limbs in Winghe's composition point toward heaven, but the viewer is, like the Hebrews themselves, free to ignore heavenly matters and choose an exhilarating coupling with Cozbi, the Midianite.

The writers of the *Tanach* of course would not endorse Winghe's art of painting with pigments, which they considered idolatry, but they did endorse the art of verbal painting. For the *Tanach* does work with the realization that ethical monotheism rests on an understanding of both psychology and artful narrative.

Relying on their readers' capacity to couple an understanding of the Hebrew mind with a thoughtful reading of sacred texts, the writers of the *Tanach* offer stories that are meant not to titillate but to educate. The vapid insurrectionist Korach and the sex-mad Zimri instruct us on why the Tenth Commandment is necessary. Human beings need repetitive reminders that their tendency to overreach, to overdo, and to blow out of proportion everything in heaven and hell undermines ethical monotheism on earth. The story of Ahab and Jezebel also teaches this lesson.

- >

IV: Jezebel's Reckless Incitement

Of all the intensely driven characters in the Bible, King Ahab's wife, Jezebel, is perhaps the most hot-headed of them all. She has even earned a place in The Oxford English Dictionary, where her name serves as a synonym for a "wicked, impudent, or abandoned woman," or for "a woman who paints her face," a conniving, masquerading harlot.

In modern English, the term "Jezebel," sometimes capitalized, sometimes not, is merely an insult, but in the Hebrew Bible *Jezebel* serves a higher purpose. The Hebrews needed to explore their own hotheaded regression back to idolatry and their embrace of strange women. Jezebel is one of the lead players in that exploration. We meet her in I Kings 16, just after Ahab takes over the kingship of Israel from his father, Omri:

> And Ahab the son of Omri did evil in the sight of the Lord above all [the kings] that were before him. And it came to pass, . . . that he took to wife Jezebel the daughter of Ethbaal king of the Zidonians, and went and served Ba'al, and worshipped him. And he reared up an altar for Baal, and worshipped him. And he reared up an altar for Baal, which he had built in Samaria. And Ahab made a grove [not a grove but a wooden idol of the Canaanite sex goddess, Ashtoreth]; and Ahab did more to provoke the Lord God of Israel to anger than all the kings of Israel that were before him.

The narrator here is careful to note that Ahab shares a character trait with his father, Omri. They are both superlative idolaters, the son worse than the father, for Ahab is a greater sinner than all the kings who came before him, presumably including his father. Ahab's name in Hebrew is *Ach-Av*, meaning brother-father; psychologically, Ahab and Omri are brothers in idolatry. Both Kings illustrate how the persistent Hebrew drift into idolatry picked up steam over time, eventually propelling the Children of Israel into disaster. When Jezebel came on board, she added an additional psychological power to that fatal voyage, for which she was now the captain.

Her first clever act, we learn in I Kings 21, was to help her husband filch a vineyard from its rightful owner, Naboth, who understandably cleaves to his family inheritance. Like Uriah, whose righteous mind was irrelevant to King David's murderous plans, Naboth wastes his honest breath on the covetous Ahab:

> And Naboth said to Ahab, The Lord forbid it me, that I should give the inheritance of my fathers unto thee. And Ahab came into his house heavy and displeased . . . . And he laid him down on his bed, and turned away his face, and would eat no bread. But Jezebel his wife came to him an said unto him, Why is thy spirit so sad, that thou eatest no bread?

Having failed to obtain his desired vineyard because its owner has an intense loyalty to his family estate, Ahab suffers a deep depression, from which he is soon rescued by Jezebel, who knows exactly how to goose-up Ahab's mood:

And Jezebel his wife said unto him, Does thou now govern the kingdom of Israel? Arise, and eat bread, and let thine heart be merry: I will give thee the vineyard of Naboth the Jezreelite. So she wrote letters in Ahab's name, and sealed them with his seal, and sent the letters unto the elders and to the nobles that were in the city, dwelling with Naboth. And she wrote in the letters, saying, Proclaim a fast, and set Naboth on high among the people: And set two men, sons of Belial before him, to bear witness against him, saying, Thou didst blaspheme God and the King. And then carry him out, and stone him that he may die.

Jezebel lures Naboth into a fatal trap by arranging a celebration of a sham day of fasting in his honor. She then hires two "sons of Belial" [i.e.,worthless men], whom she orders to falsely accuse Naboth of blasphemy, a tactic that works well.

Under the protection of Ba'al Peor, Jezebel manages to worship foreign gods, promote the erection of idols, empty out (take in vain) the meaning of Hebrew fast days, forge documents, murder Naboth, steal his vineyard, and bear false witness; she and Ahab then go on to murder most of the holy prophets in the Land, with only Elijah escaping their felonious grasp.

Ahab's desirable bride thus cheerfully violates the First, Second, Third, Sixth, Eighth, Ninth, and Tenth commandments. All this accomplished, Jezebel's husband is able to seize Naboth's vineyard under the law that grants the property of blasphemers to the King. No Queen without Jezebel's intensity could achieve this much in a year, let alone in a single day.

Because Ahab has wedded himself to Jezebel's megalomania, both he and his wife justifiably earn similar punishments, which are as intensely gruesome as their crimes. Here, in I Kings 21:19, is the punishment that the Lord asked the Prophet Elijah to deliver to Ahab:

> Thus saith the Lord, In the place where dogs licked the blood of Naboth shall dogs lick thy blood, even thine.

This cheerless decree that Ahab's sacred blood is to be licked up by dogs is followed shortly by God's similar punishment of Jezebel, the sensual bride who incited Ahab:

> And of Jezebel also spake the Lord, saying, The dogs shall eat Jezebel by the wall of Jezreel [the site of Naboth's vineyard]. Him that dieth of Ahab [those who followed Ahab's and Jezebel's idolatrous practices] in the city the dogs shall eat; and him that dieth in the field the fowls of the air shall eat. But there was none like unto Ahab, which did

sell himself to work wickedness in the sight of the Lord, whom Jezebel his wife stirred up.

For those disposed to find fault with the punitive God of the Israelites, these vicious dogs and vultures reflect the Hebrew God's perverse pleasure in gore. But this is a slanderous misreading. The *Tanach* does not display a love of bestial violence; rather, it portrays the agency in the mind that promotes the human attraction to gore. It is this condemnable agency that intensifies resentment into murder, perverts desire into thievery, and, especially, betrays monotheistic reason for the fleeting joys of Jezebel and her idolatrous minions.

What drives Jezebel? And why does Ahab permit himself to be driven by that which drives Jezebel? From whence comes the mind's capacity to intensify and thereby distort everything? How might this intensity be moderated? How might it be funneled exclusively into the enactment of ethical monotheism, or, at a minimum, away from the likes of Ba'al Peor?

In his famous novel, *Moby Dick*, Herman Melville pursues just these questions. That the hero of the novel is named Ahab and the narrator of the story is named Ishmael provides a Hebraic frame to Ahab's monomania about killing the whale that had long ago bit off one of his legs.

In the *Tanach*, the line of Ishmael is driven by the beliefs of those descendants of Abraham who rejected the more rational beliefs of Isaac and Jacob. Of course, Melville, as a

meticulous novelist, shows no interest in supporting or dis-
puting any religious conviction. He is interested in how the
human mind works, especially the irrational mind, one like
that of Ishmael, whom the God of Abraham exiled from his
paternal home, or like that of Ahab.

By presenting his tale from the perspective of Ishmael, whose name in Hebrew means "the man from God,"
Melville focuses the reader's attention on that which drives
human beings into the arms of false gods that lead us away
from the creative and meaningful life that Melville idealizes.

That Melville's Ahab in the end suffered a fate similar
to that of Ahab in the *Tanach*, the former not eaten by dogs
but by creatures at the bottom of the sea, reminds us that
the mind's hyper-active dynamics remained overwhelmingly dangerous long after the biblical Ahab was eaten by dogs.
Melville's Ishmael devotes many pages to an investigation of
cetology, or whaleology, while working as a "sub-sub librar-
ian," but he finds nothing that helps him understand the
agency that drives Ahab's monomania to kill Moby Dick
and thereby kill himself, a story that might remind us of the
biblical Samson.

Does not this whale represent that immense beast that
operates in the ship-captain's own nucleus accumbens?
Does Ahab not seek to harpoon the crazed intensity in his
own mind, fired up by that indomitable whale that serves as
the mirror image of his own unmanned self?

That all this needs psychological elucidation is part of
the message of both *Moby Dick* and the *Tanach*, both of

which open a window into the hyperactive human mind, thus illuminating the Tenth Commandment, and thereby supporting a more dignified way of using human creativity.

V: Megalomania leads to Diminution

The Children of Israel did not in fact ever moderate their self-destructive choices. At the time of the Babylonian exile in 586 BCE, they were still vacillating between commitment to their rational Lord and devotion to idolatry. As described in the Book of Kings, the narrative of decline itself dribbles away as the stature of the kings of Israel diminishes.

The Book of Kings is now divided into two parts. The second features brief attempts to reactivate the Laws of Moses, punctuated by longer episodes of idolatrous recidivism. By the end of II Kings, Jerusalem is sacked, the Temple destroyed, and most of the Jews have either been carted off to Babylonia or have fled to Egypt. The ancient Hebrews as a whole suffered the fate of Korach, Jezebel, and Ahab, severely punished for their irrational crimes.

The Children of Israel eventually realized that to undo the disastrous consequences of their slippage away from their Creator, they must restore themselves by marshaling their own creativity. The tragic story of exile was poetized by Jeremiah in his Book of Prophecy, and in the Book of Lamentations, apparently also written by Jeremiah. We will return to Jeremiah's Book of Lamentations, but the prosaic, gruesome facts of Israel's collapse are more clearly given in II Kings, where the prose is brutally sarcastic.

Here, in II Kings 23, Josiah, a righteous king of brief tenure, forces his people to celebrate a proper Passover. But then he finds that these lapsed monotheists are not righteous at all; they have even forgotten where the scroll of the Law was hidden, until Hilkiah the priest accidentally finds it:

> Surely there was not holden such a passover from the days of the judges that judged Israel, nor in all the days of the kings of Israel, nor of the kings of Judah. But in the eighteenth year of king Josiah, wherein this Passover was holden to the Lord in Jerusalem . . . the workers with familiar spirits, and the wizards, and the images, and the idols, and all the abominations that were spied in the land of Judah and in Jerusalem, did Josiah put away, that he might perform the words of law which were written in the book that Hilkiah the priest found in the house of the Lord.

The skillful narrator of this passage delays mentioning the verb that tells us what Josiah did in the eighteenth year of his reign with the wizards ("Josiah did put away"). This is likely meant to signal a prolonged process that was undertaken reluctantly. Similarly, the narrator suspends the fact that Josiah followed the Mosaic Law against necromancy only belatedly, apparently because the King's Torah scroll was only recently rediscovered. In a world where forbidden wizards are tolerated and law is accidental, the righteous King Josiah could not last long, and, in fact, he did not.

When the Egyptians, who at that time ruled the territory between the Nile and the Euphrates, charged through Israel on their way to wars in Assyria, Josiah went out to confront them; he was slain. Egyptian servants "carried him dead in a chariot from Megiddo, and brought him back to Jerusalem." At first glance we see that Josiah died because he was foolish to challenge overwhelming power. But, more importantly, he was already weakened by *his* having allowed the misplacement of the Mosaic Law, and by *his* ignoring until the last minute the intensity of his people's adoption of wizardry and necromancy.

Perhaps these Egyptian servants intended their transportation of Josiah's body back to Jerusalem as part of the celebration of their victory. But since the usual custom in ancient warfare was for the victorious power to bring the body of the conquered leader back to its own capital as part of a military celebration, our narrator, who wrote Josiah's story for the Hebrews and not the Egyptians, probably places the dead Josiah in Jerusalem as a representation of his entire moribund kingship, and as a warning to his wobbly followers to return to the sanity and sanctity of monotheism.

As the bitter end unfolds, our narrator weaves in another story about the Hebrews empty commitment to their God. The Children of Israel, having half-heartedly pretended to be followers of ethical monotheism, fall under the rule of Zedekiah, who proves to be another impostor. He is actually the uncle of the Babylonian conqueror of Israel, King Nebuchadnezzar, as we surprisingly learn in II Kings 24:12-17:

> And Nebuchadnezzar king of Babylon came against the city [Jerusalem]. And his servants did besiege it. And Jehoiachin the king of Judah went out [was exiled] to the king of Babylon . . . . And the king of Babylon took him in the eighth year of his reign. . . . And the king of Babylon made Mattaniah his father's brother king in his [Jehoiachin's] stead, and he changed his name to Zedekiah.

The all-powerful King of Babylon forced his Uncle Mattaniah (Hebrew for "God's Gift") to change his name to Zedekiah (Hebrew for "God's Justice"). This is a cruel joke on the hapless Hebrews who rejected their God. The people who pursued false gods are punished with a false king. Likewise, those who irrationally despised their own homeland were exiled to a land where they would find better reason to complain. And, after most of the Jews were expelled from Jerusalem, even Zedekiah, having double-crossed Nebuchadnezzar, was cruelly punished, as we learn in II Kings 25:

> And they slew the sons of Zedekiah before his eyes, and put out the eyes of Zedekiah, and bound him with fetters of brass, and carried him to Babylon. . . . And in the nineteenth year of

Nebuchadnezzar, King of Babylon, came Nebu-
zar-adan, captain of the guard, a servant of the King
of Babylon unto Jerusalem: And he burnt the house
of the Lord, and the kings house, and all the houses of Jerusalem, and every great man's house burnt
he with fire. And all the army of the Chaldees . . .
brake down the walls of Jerusalem. Now the rest of
the people that were left in the city . . . did Nebu-
zar-adan, the captain of the guard, carry away. But
the captain of the guard left the poor of the land to
be vinedressers and husbandmen.

Fittingly, Zedekiah, the betrayer of Nebuchadnezzar, is
punished in a way that recalls the blinding of Samson, who
betrayed his position as a *nazir*. And, to add insult upon
injury, the narrator tells us that after the majority of the
population was dispatched to Babylon, a poor remnant was
left to work as slaves in their own land, an ironic imitation
of slavery in Egypt: "The captain of the guard left the poor
of the land to be vinedressers and husbandmen."

Meanwhile the rich and the strong cried mournfully
in Babylon, their Temple destroyed, the walls of their city
demolished, and all their material wealth stripped away.
Every bowl and every teaspoon, and, especially, all their
gold and silver, was hauled away. Having abandoned their
immaterial God and His abstract commandments, they
were themselves abandoned, cast off to live in a strange land,
without the material to build another golden calf.

Our narrator in II Kings 25 goes to an extraordinary
length to list every bit of the idolatrous Hebrews' material

losses, which is only part of their punishment for having wandered into the foolishly material world of Ba'al Peor:

> And the pillars of brass that were in the house of the Lord . . . . did the Chaldees break into pieces, and carried the brass of them to Babylon. And the pots, and the shovels, and the snuffers, and the spoons, and all the vessels of brass wherewith they ministered, took they away. And the firepans, and such things as were of [pure] gold and of [pure] silver, the captain of the guard took away.

And there were more material losses, and other impositions, such as the necessity to execute some of those newly settled by the rivers of Babylon. But the grand finale to the story of the Children of Israel's punishment is the tear-jerking tale of Jehoiachin, the last legitimate King of Judah. His story closes the Book of Kings, which is essentially a summary of the ancient Hebrew's excessively driven and iteratively enacted attraction to strange women and irrational beliefs.

After being carted out of Jerusalem, King Jehoiachin rots in a Babylonian dungeon for thirty-seven years while the impostor Zedekiah rules in his place in Judah. Finally a new king, Evil-merodach (yes, *Evil*—a false cognate—is his name in Chaldean Hebrew) assumes the throne in Babylon and soon takes pity on poor Jehoiachim:

> And it came to pass in the seven and thirtieth of the captivity of Jehoiachin king of Judah . . .

that Evil-merodach king of Babylon in the year that he began to reign did lift up the head of Jehoiachin king of Judah out of prison: And he spoke kindly to him, and set his throne [chair] above the throne [chair, singular] of the kings that were with him in Babylon: And he [Jehoiachin] changed his prison garments: and he did eat bread continually before him all the days of his life. And his allowance [portion] was a continual allowance [an ongoing portion] given him of the king, a daily rate for every day, all the days of his life.

These concluding words of the Book of Kings are surprisingly melodramatic, seemingly inappropriate for a serious history of the royal line of David, of whom Jehoiachin is the last descendant. Or perhaps these concluding words are meant to be comedic.

The pleasant news delivered here is that the Davidic king is now allowed to change his clothes, gets to eat exactly the same breakfast every day for his entire life, and, best of all, he gets to sit on the highest chair in the basement where all the other kings share a single chair (that is what the grammar suggests).

There is a troubling mix of humor and pathos in this final mockery of Hebrew excess, but this is perhaps the beginning of the only possible therapy for the intense psychological mess that the Children of Israel created for themselves. Pathos and humor provide distance, distance provides a fuller perspective, and perspective provides the understanding that might help moderate folly.

Let me add here that the long line of rabbinic commentary on the Hebrews' horrifying exile to Babylonia is somewhat misleading. The rabbis treat the exile as God's punishment of the Children of Israel for having willfully broken their sacred covenant too many times. But from the material we have reviewed, we might reasonably conclude that the Hebrews were not punished but simply left as they always were, obtuse, and laughingly irrational. Like Saul, David, Solomon, and Samson, they could not hold in their minds the gifts they were given, nor could they recognize when they failed to perform. They did not rebel; they remained who they always were, a sacred people who were persistently stiff-necked, undermined by their own perverse psychology.

The comedic aspect to the Hebrews' persistent tripping over their own feet calls for a summary of the thin comedic thread that weaves through the entire *Tanach*, from Eve's ridiculously stupid encounter with the snake, to the just-freed slaves' fabrication of a golden calf to replace Moses because he was too busy on Mount Sinai, and then to Balaam's quarreling with his donkey, and then to the straddling Hebrews on Mount Carmel yelling for the appearance of their current best god, finally terminating with Jehoaichin's re-enthronement in a basement in Babylon. Along the way, we meet Naaman, the Syrian officer who comes to the bizarre understanding that the holiness of the Land of Israel resides literally in its dirt.

Dostoevsky has something to teach us along these lines. In *Crime and Punishment*, Raskolnikov, a troubled former student, commits two psychopathologic murders. He also mumbles to himself, suffers bad dreams, and behaves in such an agitated way that the authorities easily find cause to arrest and punish him. But when the novel continues to tell us more about our murderer's psychology than his punishment, we may conclude that Raskolnikov's way of thinking and acting are themselves his punishment. Whether he is killing a pawnbroker or dreaming in prison of the woman he thinks he loves passionately, he torments himself with his own comedic overdrive. In the end, his punishment is his own perverse nature, present from the beginning, almost laughable.

As in the case of Raskolnikov, the Hebrews' crime is one with their punishment. Again and again, they discarded their rational God and turned to ridiculous gods of stone and wood; and in their exile they found themselves not punished but placed where they always were, in a divine comedy. The *Tanach* thus anticipates Freud's 1905 study of *Jokes and Their Relationship to the Unconscious*. Freud, perhaps drawing on his knowledge of the Hebrew Bible (he would go on to publish *Moses and Monotheism* in 1939), understood how humor offers a way to explore troubling truths via innocent playfulness.

CHAPTER ELEVEN
Sadomasochism

I: Worse than Intensity

We have already noted the *Tanach*'s presentation of sadism in several well-crafted stories. Elkanah's fertile wife, Peninnah, takes pleasure in tormenting Hannah, the second wife, "because the Lord had shut up her womb." David sadistically cuts off Goliath's head after the giant is already dead. The Philistines enucleated Samson's eyes and planned to torture him before thousands of drunk devotees of their god. The most shocking part of the Samson story is, of course, not the Philistine's sadism, but Samson's sadomasochistic pleasure of dying in the arms of the Philistine spectators whom he slaughtered with him.

Saul twice planned to pin David to a wall with a spear, demonstrating a pleasurable outlet of violence rather than a reasonable response to danger, which was non-existent. After Saul's death, in II Samuel 21, David, too, allowed himself a sadistic outburst, granting to the Gibeonites, "not of the children of Israel," the privilege of killing one-by-one all seven of the Saul's surviving sons. Their hanging bodies were displayed to the public for five months, until Rizpah, the daughter of one of Saul's concubines, put an end to the sadistic display. She camped near the dangling bodies and prevented birds and beasts from feasting on the rotting flesh. David took pity only after he heard the report of Rizpah's attempt to moderate the sadistic acts that he himself had ordered for the purpose of fortifying an alliance with an idolatrous people whom Saul had defeated, a complicated and nasty story.

We recall that David continued his sadistic streak when he had Uriah hand-carry his own death sentence to General Joab. And we recall that Zedekiah was condemned to witness his children executed before him, and then he, like Samson, had his own eyes enucleated, so that he would never see again, assuming that this false king ever saw correctly.

II: *Tanach* and Sadomasochism

We might reasonably ask what interest propelled the authors of the *Tanach* to explore the nature of sadomasochism. Homer, of course, portrayed this psychological perversion, showing how Achilles, in Books 23 and 24 of the *Iliad*, was so overwrought by the death of his favorite,

Patroclus, that he tied the body of the Trojan hero, Hector, to his chariot and repeatedly dragged him around the perimeter of Troy. But, again, the much-honored Homer puts aside Achilles' psychology to allow the wise gods to rescue Hector's mutilated body by magically rendering it without blemish, so that he could be buried in honor. Homer may be suggesting in an indirect way, as some modern literary critics have argued, that Achilles is overwhelmed by the loss of his homosexual lover, but even if that is so, Homer leaves the understanding of Achilles' sadism to the gods.

Shakespeare seems to have had a deeper understanding of the psychological origin of sadomasochism when he, perhaps influenced by his Bible, had the gleeful, sadomasochistic daughters of Lear order that Gloucester's eyes be enucleated on stage. King Lear's faithful son-in-law, Albany, seems to understand that this kind of behavior is the expected outcome of Lear's abdication of moral authority, which releases the sadism already present in the minds of Regan, Goneril, and their lovers. Responding to a rash of sadism and gross sexual impropriety, Albany, husband of Goneril, prophesizes: "It will come,/ Humanity must perforce prey upon itself/ Like monsters of the deep." The wise Shakespeare anticipates Freud by 300 years in implying that the "monsters of the deep" are not sharks in the deep blue sea but forces that reside in the deep of the human mind, for Albany is speaking these words about his own wife's sadism.

Modern psychology definitively placed the origins of sadomasochism in the mind. Freud, for example, localized sadomasochism in the unconscious jungle of infantile memories of pleasure, pain, and fear. Every child, Freud reasoned in his three essays on the development of adult sexuality, enjoyed the pleasure of sucking nourishment and the near simultaneous pain of not being able to control hunger or other bodily discomfort. Freud added to these childhood traumas his idea of the "primal scene," the virtually universal experience of misinterpreting the meaning of hearing one's parents in the fearful act of sexual intercourse. These infantile pleasures and pains compose a primitive version of sexuality, which should mature into a healthy adult sexuality. But, said Freud, when normal maturation falters, sadomasochism expresses sexuality in its primitive form.

The *Tanach* does not of course express any opinion about these exotic ideas, but it does view sadomasochism as one possible tendency of the human mind, but not the only one. Juxtaposed to the account of David having ordered the Gibeonites to hang Saul and all seven of his sons and let them rot on the rope, is the story of David's change of heart after he hears of the merciful acts of Rizpah, Saul's daughter, who had camped near the hanging corpses to protected them from becoming food for the circling predators, as described in II Samuel 21:

> And it was told David what Rizpah the daughter of Aiah, the concubine of Saul, had done. And David went and took the bones of Saul and the bones of Jonathan his son; and they gathered the bones of them that were hanged. And the bones of

Saul and Jonathan his son buried they in . . . the sepulcher of Kish his [Saul's] father: and they performed all that the king [David] commanded. And after that God was entreated for the land.

Without knowing any formal psychology, the author of this passage shows how a change of perspective can move David from a sadistic hanging of Saul's sons to an understanding of what the God of Israel demands. In ancient Israel, righteous behavior depended not on the sexual favors of a concubine, like Aiah, but on the mercy of her daughter, Rizpah, whose name means, *a place to stand*. Only she, on this occasion, has the standing to move David to behave mercifully.

The authors of the *Tanach* portray mercy and sadism as part of a psychological spectrum, each at opposite ends of the same mind, which is capable of acting on either, as David himself understood from his own experience. Here in Psalm 86, the poet sings about his hellish mind, or "heart," and how it has matured:

I will praise thee, O Lord, my God, with all my heart . . . For great is thy mercy toward me: and thou has delivered my soul from the lowest hell.

In the context of David's history, this is not the language of a pious sermon, but a skillful analysis of the Hebrew mind's persistent failure to distinguish a merciful God from Molech's hell.

The prophet Micah makes this distinction easily. He will walk humbly with his God while others store their minds with wickedness:

> What doth the Lord require of thee but to do justly, to love mercy, and to walk humbly with thy God. . . . Are there yet treasures of wickedness in the house of the wicked?

David learned these precepts the hard way, in the lowest rungs of hell.

The composers of the *Tanach* found idolatrous sadomasochism so antagonistic to monotheism's sanctification of human life that they prohibited even mildly malign practices, such as cutting oneself as a relief from mourning, and tattooing oneself. Let us look again at Leviticus 19:28:

> Ye shall not make any cuttings to your flesh for the dead, nor print [*ka-ah-ka*, in Hebrew] any marks upon you: I am the Lord.

Like the English word *tattoo*, the Hebrew equivalent, *ka-ah-ka*, telegraphs a mindless tapping sound to mock treating the human body sadistically, as if it were a non-living idol, ready to be decorated.

CHAPTER TWELVE
REASON

I: REASON AS A NECESSARY CAPACITY OF MIND

For millennia, human architects and engineers used reason to work through complex problems, such as to how to build a pyramid so that all four edges would meet precisely at the apex. Aqueducts had to run smoothly down hill and terminate exactly in the right place. Temples in Mayan city-states were built so that the rising sun appeared in a small window at a precise moment on the longest day of the year.

Eventually, after long neglect, philosophers posed the obvious questions. What exactly was the capacity of mind that allowed men to solve abstract problems? Humans could probably deduce that wolves learned how to hunt by imitating the tactics of successful packs, but what capacity of the mind, wherever it might be, allowed humans to reason, to create that which never before existed, to detect the flaws of an argument, and to design a ship sturdy enough to carry cargo, and not sink in stormy seas? How did the human mind reveal truth?

In the Fourth century BCE, Aristotle began the exploration of these questions. With no understanding of the physiology of the brain, he was left with a qualitative description of what the mind's principles of logical thinking must be. In *Nicomachean Ethics* I.13, he observed that men possess a *logon echon*, a rational principal that lifts humans above plants, which are governed only by a nutritive drive, and animals, which are governed by nutritive instinct and by primitive drives, such as reproduction.

That a rational principle governs human beings led Aristotle into the abstract domain of logic. This, in turn, became the foundation of formal logic, and that led to the great advancement of information technology today. How the human brain manages rational thought is still a mystery, but Aristotle assumed that some mechanism must exist to carry out the logical acts he describes. Thus Aristotle provided the foundation on which future scholars explored the nature of reason, from Euclid, to Aquinas, to Descartes, to Kant, and to more modern philosophers.

Let us take a glimpse at Kant's thoughts about reason in his "Refutation of Idealism":

> Whether this or that experience is not mere imagination must be ascertained according to its particular determinations and its coherence with all

the criteria of actual experience. . . . The law of reason to seek unity is necessary, since without it we would have no reason, and without that, no coherent use of understanding, and lacking that, no sufficient mark of empirical truth.

Euclidian axioms must be coherent with each other and produce no proofs that contradict other proofs. There must be a unity of methodology and a unity of findings. If this were not true, one could not reasonably proceed with further propositions about triangles, at least not in Euclidian geometry. Similarly, the *Tanach* is careful to demonstrate that the world cannot be reasonably understood as having been created by multiple gods who demand adherence to multiple systems of understanding.

Monotheism is inherently coherent from its inception. A society that is most likely to survive will cleave to a unified vision of a just and meaningful life. A coherent idea is promulgated throughout the *Tanach*, following, as it happens, the demands of unity and coherence of Kantian philosophy. For monotheism is by its nature unified and coherent.

The *Tanach*, of course, never intended to undertake a formal analysis of the nature of reason or logic. But because the Hebrews often failed to distinguish the rationality of monotheism from the irrationality of idolatry, they forced to explore the difference between how they were supposed to think and how their neighbors thought.

We have seen the Tanach's demonstration of various psychopathologies that undermine rational thinking. Saul's reason is twisted by psychosis, David's by a manic-depressive disorder, Samson by a wobbly executive function, and Solomon by allowing the Queen of Sheba and his 300 concubines to corrupt his reason. But what exactly is reason? What process allows the mind to distinguish the rational from the irrational?

The *Tanach*, of course knows no modern neuroscience. But it *does* address the nature of reason, a subject about which no idolater has ever inquired. Because the *Tanach* often resembles a literary text more than a philosophical or even theological discussion, one easily misses its small contribution to the nature of reason. Let us then look at four biblical vignettes that help reveal the difference between rational and irrational thinking. My discussion of Eve, Noah, Abraham's and Sarah's laughter, and Abraham's debate with God likely run afoul of more hallowed readings, but I will let the *Tanach* speak for itself.

II: The Snake Debates with Eve

The story of Adam and Eve was long ago moved into the realm of Christian sin ("In Adam's fall, we sinned all"), but the Hebrews likely saw it as an illustration of how easily human reason is corrupted. Here is part of the familiar story in Genesis 2:25, continuing into 3:1-6:

And they were both naked [*Aroomim*, naked, plural]. Now the serpent was more subtle [*Aroom*, crafty] than any beast of the field, which the Lord God made. And he said unto the woman, Yea, hath God said, You shall not eat of every tree of the garden? And the woman said unto the Serpent, We may eat of the fruit of the trees of the garden: But of the fruit of the tree which is in the midst of the garden, Ye shall not eat of it, lest ye die. And the serpent said unto the woman, Ye shall not surely die: For God doth know that the day ye eat thereof, then your eyes shall be open, and ye shall see as gods, knowing good and evil. And when the woman saw that the tree was good for food, and that it was pleasant [*nechmad*, related to the word "covet"] to the eyes, and a tree to be desired to make one wise, she took the fruit thereof, and did eat, and gave also unto her husband with her; and he did eat.

This introduction to the nature of the serpent focuses not on his diabolic blasphemy, but on what the Greeks would call his sophistry, the capacity to use argument not to find the truth but to support a falsehood. The serpent is cunning and wily, a stand-in for human sophistry, a corrupter of reason, not a sinner. He allows the woman to repeat verbatim what God has told her, and then he perverts what God said, which leads Eve into the realm of literalism. In that realm, Eve finds that the fruit of the tree is no longer a symbol of God's Law, but a thing in itself, "good for food." And her blunted perception can no longer understand an abstract prohibition, registering no more than something "pleasant to the eyes," or, in Hebrew, something worth coveting (*nechmad*). She is a forerunner of the blind spies who see nothing of value in the land as an idea. What they bring back is food.

The snake promises Eve that she will be "wise" if she eats the apple, but she shows no understanding of what wisdom is or why it will improve her current situation. And, of course it doesn't. She thinks that it is more reasonable to follow the dictates of her own literalistic mind than to accept the superior wisdom of the Lord.

She and Adam are both described as naked (*aroomim*}, which happens to be the same word used to describe the serpent's guile (*aroom*). All three of these characters share the same metaphoric nakedness that renders their irrationality obvious, and that is exactly what is going to make the serpent's and the young couple's lives miserable:

> And the Lord said unto the serpent , . . . I will put enmity between thou and the woman, and between thy seed and his [a descendant's] seed; it [the enmity] shall bruise thy head, and thou shall bruise his heel. Unto the woman he said, I will greatly multiply thy sorrow in conception; in sorrow thou shalt bring forth children; and thy desire shall be to thy husband, and he shall rule over thee. . . . And unto Adam he said, . . . cursed be the ground for thy sake . . . . Thorns also and thistles shall it bring forth to thee.

If we see the serpent as a sophist, Eve as the first human to be duped into irrationality, and her husband as the second, then this passage is neither a revelation of Christianity's original sin, nor a support of the modern feminist claim that men blame women unfairly for everything that goes wrong. This story, in the context of the Israelites' irrational attraction to idolatrous reasoning, is a warning not to be led astray by their fatal attraction to foreign gods, represented here by the snake. This interpretation best explains why this story of Adam and Eve's faulty reasoning occurs early in the *Tanach*. Sin became a central problem later, after the giving of the Law on Mount Sinai, the acceptance of which depended on the Hebrews' capacity to reason at a level higher than that which the foolish Adam and Eve could attain. For the ancient Hebrews, the primal flaw was not sin but stupidity.

III: Noah Does an Experiment And then Gets Drunk

The story of Noah and his ark has so many absurd details that it has become something of a religious fairy tale, with Noah's dove having become an emblem of Jesus, and God's rainbow a promise of peace on earth. The story of an ark capable of accommodating every species of beetle, bird, and bison along with enough food to sustain them for five months on a turbulent sea cannot be taken literally.

What can be taken seriously are two details that pertain to Noah's capacity to reason. His ability to run an experiment (to determine when it is appropriate to land this overloaded boat) speaks well of his ability to reason, but his second plan, to grow grapes and get drunk as soon as possible, calls his rational capacity into question, which just happens to be a reflection of the Hebrew's chronic problematic reasoning.

All through the *Tanach*, the Hebrews can understand that their commitment to ethical monotheism is reasonable, but they cannot reliably honor it. Noah has been chosen to be the captain of this redemptive ship because he, like the Hebrews themselves, have "found grace in the eyes of the Lord," and, just like the Hebrews, he bungles his mission, as we see in Genesis 7 & 8:

> And God saw that the wickedness of man was great in the earth, and every imagination of the thoughts of his heart [better: "every form of his reasoning"] was only evil continuously [*kol ha-yom*, all day long] . . . . And the Lord said, "I will destroy man whom I have created from the face of the earth; both man and beast, and the creeping thing, and the fowls of the air; for it repenteth me that I have made them.

That the Creator repents that He made a mistake in creating mankind is not meant as an admission of fallibility but as a metaphoric way of emphasizing that the irrational "thoughts" of mankind at the time of Noah were an "evil" that would not be tolerated, especially among the Children of Israel, for whom Noah's story is told. That God insists on destroying even the animals is not an expression of contempt for innocent life, but a measure of the depth of mankind's irrational thinking. All living things must be destroyed in this story because man has corrupted the entire creation by his failure to behave reasonably. Intense crimes require intense punishments, a prominent literary trope in the *Tanach*, especially, as we saw, in the stories of Korach and Zimri.

Noah's story continues:

> But Noah found grace in the eyes of the Lord. . . . And God said unto Noah, . . . Make thee an ark of gopher wood; rooms shalt thou make in the ark, and shalt pitch it within and without with pitch. . . . Of clean beasts, and of beasts that were not clean, and of fowls, and every thing that creepeth upon the earth, there went unto the ark two and two unto Noah into the ark, the male and the female. . . . And the selfsame day entered Noah, and Shem, and Ham, Japheth, the sons of Noah, and Noah's wife, and the three wives of his sons with them, into the ark. . . . And the waters prevailed upon the earth an hundred and fifty days. . . . And it came to pass at the end of forty days [after the waters began subsiding] that Noah . . . . sent forth a dove from him to see if the waters were dried up from the face of the ground; But the dove found no rest

for the sole of her foot, and she returned to the ark
. . . . And he stayed another seven days; and again
he sent forth the dove out of the ark; and the dove
came back to him in the evening; and, lo, in her
mouth was an olive leaf plukt off; so Noah knew
that the waters abated from the earth. . . . And
God spake unto Noah, saying, Go forth of the ark,
thou and thy wife, and thy sons, and thy sons' wives
with thee. Bring forth with thee every living thing
that is with thee.

The cognitively apt Noah was able to follow God's
detailed blueprint of how to build an ark, and on his own he
devised an experiment to determine when it was safe to go
ashore. But soon after landing he loses his way. His sons
find him drunk in his tent:

And Noah began to be an husbandman, and
he planted a vineyard: And he drank of the wine,
and was drunken; and he was uncovered within his
tent. And Ham, the father of the Canaanites, saw
the nakedness of his father *[ervat aviv*, Hebrew
for viewing the naked vulnerability of ones father,
a taboo], and told his two brothers without . . .
. And Noah awoke from his wine and knew what
his younger son had done unto him. And he said,
Cursed be Canaan; a servant of servants shall he be
unto his brethren.

This story about Canaatite Ham's dishonoring of his
father adds another justification, beyond God's promise, for

the Israelite's future displacement of the Canaanites. But the story also contains a deeper meaning. That Noah is irrationally drunk is bad enough, but even worse is that his son Ham has violated a significant taboo, not obvious to a modern reader. Exposing a father's nakedness is, like bestiality and incest, on the list of forbidden violations of decency, as numerated in Leviticus 20.

In the Hebrew view, decency is part of the respect owed to ones father and mother, as stated in the Fifth Commandment. Honoring ones father and mother signals a respect for God, the Father of Creation, without which one cannot survive long in the Promised Land, or anywhere else, according to the second part of the Commandment, which is often ignored:

> Honour thy father and thy mother: that thy days be long upon the land which the Lord thy God giveth thee."

The Hebrews believed that their honoring their fathers and mothers signaled their greater responsibility to honor their Lord. Their inability to abide by God's Law was as unreasonable as getting drunk, having sex with animals, or chasing after strange women and foreign gods. At least Noah didn't have enough time to get further into irrationality than drunkenness, leaving intact the possibility that his descendants might be able to adapt their forefather's ark-building skills to the more complicated task of building an ethical civilization.

IV: Abraham and Sarah Mock
God's Ridiculous Promise

Two of the many puzzling scenes in the *Tanach* occur early in the story of Abraham's and Sarah's earnest endeavor to establish themselves in the Promised Land. These stories seem deliberately structured to make the fulfillment of God's covenant with Abraham appear highly unlikely, even risible. In fact, both Abraham and Sarah cannot keep themselves from laughing!

As we learn in Genesis 17:15-17, at age 99 Abraham circumcises himself, as God has commanded, and soon thereafter God tells him that Sarah, age 90, will bear him within the year a son named Isaac, who will supersede Ishmael, the son who was born to his concubine, Hagar. This birth assures that the seed of Abraham and Sarah will eventually become as plentiful as the stars in the sky:

> And God said unto Abraham, As for Sarah thy wife, . . . I will bless her, and give thee a son also [in addition to Ishmael] of her: yea, I will bless her, and she shall be a mother of nations; kings of people shall be of her. Then Abraham fell upon his face and laughed, and said in his heart, Shall a child be born unto him that is an hundred years old? And shall Sarah, that is ninety years old, bear?

The ancient rabbis, of course, could not accept that there could be any levity in Abraham's righteous mind, and they assumed, as did Rashi, that Abraham must be rejoicing, not mocking, even though the Hebrew is quite clear that he laughed.

And the Hebrew is quite clear that Sarah laughed, too. Even Rashi had to agree that Sarah laughed, because God chastises her for laughing when she tries to deny her obviously disrespectful act, as we see in Genesis 18. When three angels, disguised as wayfarers, appear to Abraham and Sarah in their campsite in Genesis 18:9-15, Sarah hears one of the angels confirm with Abraham that she will soon give birth:

> And he said to him [Abraham], Where is Sarah, thy wife? And he said, Behold, in the tent. And he [the appointed angel] said, I will certainly return to the according to the time of life [i.e., the time of pregnancy], and, lo, Sarah, thy wife shall have a son. . . . Now Abraham and Sarah were old and well stricken in age; and it ceased to be with Sarah after the manner with women. Therefore Sarah laughed within her self, saying, After I am waxed old shall I have pleasure, my lord being old, also? And the Lord said unto Abraham, Wherefore did Sarah laugh? . . . Is there anything too hard for the Lord? At the time appointed I will return unto thee, according to the time of life, and Sarah shall have a son. Then Sarah denied, saying, I laughed not; for she was afraid. And He [the Lord] said, Nay, thou didst laugh.

This inquiring angel of course knows where Sarah is, but he maintains his human pose, presumably looking for a natural human response. Rashi and other respected commentators go around and around about this complicated rigmarole about laughing or not laughing, mocking or rejoicing, being grateful for or being merely astonished by this miraculous blessing. All this meandering speculation misses what I believe to be the central problem with these stories. Why are they present at all? Why are the very first steps toward the realization of the Abrahamic covenant made to appear so risible, even to the central characters?

By calling these bursts of laughter simple expressions of astonishment (*meheemoot*, in Hebrew), Rashi avoids confronting problematic passages that characterize the foundation of the Hebrew nation as a laughable pipe-dream. The reader has been led to expect stories more like the one told in Genesis 14, where a vigorous and younger Abraham rescues his nephew, Lot, as he defeats a league of nations that had overwhelmed Canaan and rode away with many captives. Why is this vigorous Abraham not the one who receives the announcement that he will soon have a son and begin the fulfillment of the covenant? Why bother with a laughing, aged patriarch and a snickering, post-menopausal matriarch? Why not have Sarah (whose name means *princess*) receive the good news when she was so beautiful that Abraham had to introduce her as his sister in Genesis 20 to prevent his being killed by the powerful Abimelech, who would then take the attractive princess to be his own wife?

Presumably, there is a reason for placing the announcement of Isaac's birth in a gerontologic setting, in which Abraham and Sarah, as escapees from an irrational, child-sacrificing civilization, would by their very nature likely burst into laughter at the absurd prospect of producing a child at their age. And that reason is likely, in the context of the *Tanach* as a whole, a recognition that the ancient Hebrews were in for a long journey before they could stop making a mockery of themselves. The Abrahamic covenant is simply not easy to grasp.

To demonstrate that Abraham is indeed up to the challenge, he is immediately called upon to demonstrate his capacity to be the patriarch of ethical monotheism.

V: Abraham Debates with God

Over many centuries, Chapter 18 of Genesis has elicited many commentaries on Abraham's startling challenge of God, who intends to obliterate Sodom and its four sister cities without distinguishing sinners from the righteous. Ibn Ezra finds Abraham's challenge of God's sense of justice inexplicably wrong-headed: "How is it possible for the Judge of all the earth to act unjustly?" Most commentators agree that Abraham is testing God as he slowly lowers the number of righteous Sodomites (first 50, then 45, and then, after several more negotiated steps down, to 10 righteous souls) that would suffice to spare the five immoral cities.

But God, of course, needs no test. It is the Patriarch of a rational people who must demonstrate to his descendants that he can reason, even at his advanced age, at a sufficiently high level to understand the rational laws of a rational

God. The demonstration of Abraham's capacity to negotiate in good faith is what distinguishes his monotheism from Lot's irrational participation in sodomite customs, including incestuous childbearing with his daughters.

Perhaps this perspective allows the best answer to Ibn Ezra's reasonable objection. Let us then look more closely at Abraham's negotiations with God in Genesis 18:

> And the Lord said, Shall I hide from Abraham that thing which I will do; Seeing that Abraham shall surely become a great and mighty nation, and all the nations of the earth shall be blessed in him? For I know him, that he will command his children and his household after him, and they shall keep the way of the Lord, to do justice and judgment. . . . And the Lord said, Because the cry of Sodom and Gomorrah is great and their sin is very grievous, I will go down now, and see whether they have done altogether according to the cry of it.

Presumably God did not need to "go down now" to see for Himself whether the cry from Sodom and Gomorrah represented reality. But it is necessary to demonstrate to the often-irrational Hebrews what a rational investigation entails. This seemingly unnecessary verse about God conducting an in-person investigation is to be set in contrast with the way Lot and his wife handle their escape from Sodom in Genesis 19:15-22:

And when the morning arose, then the angels hastened Lot, saying, Arise take thy wife, and thy two daughters, which are here; lest thou be consumed in the iniquity of the city. . . . And it came to pass, when they had brought them forth abroad, that he said, Escape for thy life; look not behind thee, neither stay thou in all the plain; escape to the mountain, lest thou be consumed. And Lot said unto them, Oh, not so my Lord: Behold now, thy servant hath found grace in they sight, and though hast magnified thy mercy, which thou has shewed unto me in saving my life; and I cannot escape to the mountain, lest some evil take me, and I die. Behold now, this city is near to flee unto, and it is a little one: Oh, let me escape thither, {is it not a little one?) and my soul shall live. . . . Therefore the name of the city was called Zoar [i.e., Little].

Like Abraham, Lot thinks it reasonable to negotiate with God, but he doesn't actually negotiate. He tells God what the most reasonable plan should be, based on an unfounded assertion that he might die up on the mountain. But Sodom is in the Dead Sea valley, 1200 feet below sea level, and the Ancient Hebrews thought of the hills above the valley as the site of civilization, as in Bethlehem, whose name means the House of Food (much later the generic Semitic word, *lechem*, bifurcated into the Hebrew word for bread, *lechem*, and the similar Arabic word for meat, *lacham*). Further, Lot's justification of his preference is the fact that he chose a *small* city, a claim that he repeats. This is a ridiculous and irrelevant justification for overruling his Lord.

Nevertheless, God, as is His wont, allows Lot to choose, as we see in Genesis 19:21-26:

And He said unto him [Lot], See, I have accepted thee concerning this thing also, that I will not overthrow this city, for the which thou has spoken. . . . Then the Lord rained upon Sodom and upon Gomorrah brimstone and fire from the Lord out of heaven: And He overthrew those cities, and all the plain, and all the inhabitants of the cities, and that which grew upon the ground. But his wife looked back from behind him [Lot], and she became a pillar of salt.

Though told not to look back as she flees from Sodom, Lot's wife does exactly that. Being turned into a pillar of salt may seem an excessive punishment, something that does not resemble the good Lord's justice; it rather mirrors Ovid's story about an angry god turning a man into a flower. But we are here in the Hebraic realm of a symbolic punishment for an irrational disobedience of the rational Lord, a crime deserving of a severe punishment. God Himself went down to inspect the evil ways of Sodom, but Lot's wife makes a mockery of God's wanting to validate what He has heard about Sodom's abominations. In glancing back at burning Sodom, Lady Lot establishes rubbernecking as an irrational equivalent to God's rational inspection, which of course leads to a disaster that could have been avoided had she left the matter in God's wise hands.

And of course Lot looks back, too. He soon realizes that his choice to flee to Zoar was not so wise, and so he returns to God's original plan. Bur he corrupts that, too. He winds up living in a mountain cave with his daughters, who misperceive the fires around them as the end of the world. To rescue their family's line, they decide to get their father drunk and have him inseminate them, as told in Genesis 19:28-32:

> And he [Lot] looked back at Sodom and Gomorrah, and to all the land of the plain, and behold, and lo, the smoke of the country went up as the smoke of a furnace. . . . And Lot went out of Zoar, and dwelt in the mountain, and his two daughters went with him; for he feared to live in Zoar; and he dwelt in a cave, he and his two daughters. And the firstborn said unto the younger, Our father is old, and there is not a man in the earth to come in unto us after the manner of all the earth: Come let us make our father drink wine, and we will lie with him, that we may preserve the seed of our father.

These two brilliant daughters of Lot soon gave birth, the firstborn to Moab, the progenitor of the Moabites, the younger to Ben-Ammi (son of my people), the progenitor of the Ammonites, all enemies of the Israelites (even if Ben-Ammi carries a favorable Hebrew name). Lot, his daughters, and their descendants all lacked reason, and they soon settled into disaster, either defeated in the field, or irreparably sunk into a cave of incest and ineptitude. Recall that Lot had earlier offered his daughters as substitutes when a few of Sodom's louts knocked on his door and demanded homosexual satisfaction.

Lot's poor reasoning serves as a foil for Abraham's more effective thinking. Abraham outsmarts his nephew when they have to separate their households because their shepherds are quarreling. Abraham gives Lot the first choice of destination, because it doesn't matter what he chooses. Abraham knows that God has already granted him the entire country. And when Lot chooses Sodom because it has green pastures, Abraham quietly accepts Lot's decision, understanding that his nephew, who is oblivious both to Sodom's lewd reputation and to the covenantal meaning of the Land, will likely suffer the fate of Sodom.

Similarly, Abraham outsmarts Ephron when he wishes to acquire from this Hittite his Cave of *Machpelah* as a burial place for his deceased wife, Sarah.At first Ephron is willing to give the cave to the needy stranger, but when Abraham insists on buying it, Ephron, sniffing a chance to make a killing, demands an exorbitant price. What Ephron cannot see is that by paying this high price Abraham secures a foothold in the Land whose entirety he has already been promised.

The *Tanach* repetitively demonstrates that without reason the Hebrews would find themselves in a sea of idolatrous irrationality, but if they allowed themselves to be governed by monotheistic reason they might just survive on the Land that they had been given. The ancient Hebrews came close to articulating Kant's famous dictum about living in a society without a rational foundation: "We would have no reason, and without that, no coherent use of understanding, and lacking that, no sufficient mark of empirical truth."

CHAPTER THIRTEEN
JOSEPH AND THE INTERPRETATION OF DREAMS

I: JOSEPH'S AGGRESSIVE DREAMS

After Freud published his *The Interpretation of Dreams* on the eve of the Twentieth century, the understanding of dreams moved out of the realm of myth, superstition, fortune-telling, and oracles. Ancient dream interpreters believed that a dream was either a sacred message from one god or another, or was a veiled prophecy that did not necessarily pertain to the dreamer's own mind.

In contrast, Freud correctly argued that dreams arose out of a specific dreamer's mind and reflected the concerns of that mind. Though virtually all psychologists agree with this general proposition, the details of Freud's analysis of dreams are not easily accepted. Because the meaning of a dream is usually opaque both to the dreamer and his doctor, many therapists remained in doubt about the accuracy of any interpretation of a dream based on Freud's peculiar code.

Freud insisted that the themes of a dream were disguised in order to protect the privacy of the delicate thoughts and feelings hidden in the dreamer's unconscious mind. Since it was not easy to decode what exactly those delicate matters might be, many other schools of dream interpretations arose, with one contradicting another, much like the competing views of the ancient gods.

But at least all psychotherapists agree that a dream requires an interpretation, and that interpretation must fit the psychological situation of the dreamer. And that means that a convincing interpretation of a dream must be coherent, with all its parts fitting together, like a well-wrought poem.

Long before Freud, the Torah presented Joseph's dreams as creations of Joseph's own mind. But the Torah did not regard Joseph's dreams as shadows projected from his unconscious mind, but revelations of his cleverness, his ability to see clearly and reason his way through what he understood, as we shall see in a moment. Nor did the Torah present Joseph's dreams as fulfillments of forbidden wishes, as Freud attempted to do with great difficulty, especially in the case of nightmares. However, the Torah did anticipate Freud in that it recognized that a successful interpretation of a dream must integrate all its details into a coherent, unified whole, like monotheism itself.

This approach is clearly seen in the way that Torah presents Joseph's two, youthful dreams, as recorded in Genesis 37:2-8:

> Joseph, being seventeen years old, was feeding the flock with his brethren . . . . and Joseph brought unto his father their evil report [i.e. Joseph brought to his father a harsh account of his brothers' inappropriate behavior [*deebatam*]. Now Israel [synonymous with Jacob] loved Joseph more than all his children, . . . and he made him a coat of many colours. And when his brethren saw that their father loved him more than all his brethren, they hated him, and could not speak peacefully unto him. And Joseph dreamed a dream, and he told it to his brethren: and they hated him yet the more. And Joseph said unto them, Hear, I pray you, this dream which I have dreamed: For, behold, we were binding sheaves in the field, and lo, my sheaf arose, and also stood upright; and, behold your sheave stood round about, and made obeisance to my sheaf.

Joseph's dream is not a message from an angel or God, nor a prophecy about his future grandeur, but a reflection of how he feels about his brothers' hostility toward him. His mind is canny about the way it uses the dream story to shame his brothers for their malevolent treatment, but he also foolishly raises the temperature of his brother's hatred to the point that he almost gets himself killed. The dream is so blatantly hostile that one might wonder if Joseph had consciously decided to tuck his aggressive self-aggrandizement

into the ancient belief that dreams came from the mysterious gods, hoping thereby to evade his brothers' wrath. In
any case, with his immature executive function, he misses
the clear and present danger of further antagonizing his
already-inflamed brothers.

Having misread the impact of his dream, Joseph immediately foists another hostile dream on his brothers:

> And his brethren said to him, Shalt thou indeed
> reign over us? . . . And they hated him the more
> for his dreams, and for his words. And he dreamed
> yet another dream, and told it [to] his brethren, and
> said, Behold, I have dreamed a dream more; and,
> behold, the sun and the stars made obeisance to me.
> And he told it to his father and to his brethren, and
> his father rebuked him.

Jacob understands that his own love for Joseph, his
having blessed this prince of sons with a sumptuous mul-
ti-colored cloak, and Joseph's own tattling about his brothers' misdeeds, have driven the bothers to a dangerous hatred.
He thus warns Joseph that his clever dreams have likely put
him into grave danger. Jacob is so worried about what his
eleven angry sons might be planning that he rather foolishly sends Joseph to find out what the brothers are doing in
Shechem.

But Joseph does not find his brothers in Shechem. He
is told by a man whose path he happens to cross that his
brothers have departed for Dotan, a town near the coast, on

the caravan route, far from the hill country around Shechem. The early rabbis guessed that this man who informs Joseph about the whereabouts of his brothers was the angel Gabriel. But the story's emphasis on Joseph's high intelligence, his fitness for his future job of managing the fortunes of Egypt, suggests that he is the kind of man who reliably finds his way out of a jam. Thus, the random man on Joseph 's otherwise quiet road to Shechem is likely a personification of Joseph's own capacity to arrive at rapid insights based on prior experience. Most likely, Joseph reasoned from his prior observation of his brothers that they had slipped away to Dotan because it was on the caravan route, where prostitutes plied their trade.

And indeed that is where Joseph finds them, likely providing him with more salacious material to report to his father. But young Joseph has underestimated his danger. When the brothers catch sight of him in Genesis 45:4-7, they say:

> Behold, the dreamer cometh. Let us slay him and cast him [his body] into some pit, and we will say, Some evil beast has devoured him.

But the eldest brother, Reuben, hoping to rescue his brother and "deliver him to his father again," says to his brothers, "Let us not kill him, ... Shed no blood." So, Joseph is thrown into a waterless pit, but before Reuben could return to the pit, Judah, having spotted a caravan of Ishmaelites, suggests a profitable way to avoid the sin of Cain.

"What profit is it if we slay our brother and conceal his blood … Let us sell him to the Ishmaelites, and let not our hand be upon him, for he is our brother and our flesh." But along come the Midianites, and it is they who sell Joseph to the Ishmaelites and garner twenty pieces of silver for their trouble.

An attentive Hebrew reader would want to know why the narrative of Joseph's arrival in Egypt required such a complicated prologue. Jacob foolishly sends his favorite son into the maw of disaster; then the enflamed brothers plan to kill the haughty dreamer and throw his body into a pit; but Reuben persuades his brothers to throw the living Joseph into the pit, where he will likely die from thirst; but Reuben can secretly rescue him and return him to Jacob; in the meantime, Judah plans to sell Joseph to the Ishmaelites; however, the Midianites intervene and close the sale to the Ishmaelites; and, finally, the rejected line of Abraham bring Joseph down to Egypt and sell the handsome lad to Potiphar, who makes him his steward, a position that allows Joseph to marshal his intelligence and thrive.

Why was this complicated prologue to Joseph's arrival in Egypt necessary? The plot does require the false accusations of Potiphar's wife to get Joseph thrown into jail, where he meets the Butler and the Baker, which leads to his being summoned to the palace to interpret Pharaoh's dreams, which he accomplishes so impressively that Pharaoh raises him to the pinnacle of power in Egypt. Given the fact that the plot of Joseph's story is sufficiently complicated once he arrives in Egypt, why do we need all those twists and turns just to get Joseph into Egypt?

The ancient rabbis had much to say about individual details of Joseph's journey to Egypt, but they say nothing about the need for such a bizarre itinerary. Perhaps the rabbis found this issue unimportant because it was more literary than spiritual. But for the literary People of the Book, their spiritual capacities and literary capacities were interdependent. From this perspective, we can see a meaning to all these prefatory complications: Only coherent reasoning can manage the chance events and impenetrable dreams that commonly overwhelm the human mind.

Once established as the successful steward of Potiphar's estate, the handsome Joseph catches the eye of his lord's wife, who tries to seduce him. Though he flees from her, leaving his cloak behind in his haste, she alleges that he tried to rape her, abandoning his cloak only because she had clutched it while defending herself. This false accusation, supported by the cloak as evidence, soon lands Joseph in prison, where he meets two other dreamers, Pharaoh's baker and his butler. From his own experience, he knows that a dream is the product of the mind of the dreamer, and with this understanding, the intelligent interpreter, now wised up after his faulty reading of his brothers' vitriol, goes to work, first on the butler's dream in Genesis 40:5-13:

> And they said unto him, We have dreamed a
> dream, and there is no interpreter of it. And Joseph
> said unto them, Do not interpretations belong to

God? Tell me them I pray you. And the chief butler told his dream to Joseph, and said to him, In my
dream, behold, a vine was before me; And in the
vine were three branches: and it was as though it
budded, and her blossoms shot forth; and the clus-
ters thereof brought forth ripe grapes: And Pharaoh's cup was in my hand: and I took the grapes,
and pressed them into Pharaoh's cup, and I gave the
cup unto Pharaoh's hand.

Now any professional who has worked with patients
to reveal the meaning of their dreams, knows that dreams
do not proceed in a logical and orderly fashion, as does the
butler's dream. But the narrative of the butler's dream is
not in this case composed to reveal what is on the butler's
mind (we have already been told that he is worried about
his fate) but what kind of mind Joseph possesses. Does he
have the wherewithal to deduce what is likely to happen to
the butler? Can he observe astutely and come to a rational
conclusion?

That is exactly what Joseph does, and that is probably why this story is in the Torah. For the Hebrew God
demands not that His people become psychoanalysts but
rational adherents to Mosaic Law. When Joseph announces
that "interpretations belong to God," the context makes his
true meaning clear: the capacity to make a rational interpretation derives from a civilization enriched by a rational
God.

From this point of view, it is not difficult for him to
understand from his close attention to the details of butler's

dream that the innocent man radiates an enthusiastic love for serving his Pharaoh, that he is eager to serve Pharaoh again, to put the royal cup into his royal hand. And the butler's vision of a vine bursting into bloom is also a fitting image of his joy in a possible return to faithful service.

Since Joseph possesses the capacity to read what he sees, he comes to the right conclusion:

> And Joseph said unto him, This is the interpretation of it: The three branches are three days: Yet within three days shall Pharaoh lift up thine head, and restore the unto thy place, and thus shalt deliver Pharaoh's cup unto his hand, after the former manner when thou wast his butler.

Joseph's rational interpretation is based on a careful reading of the Butler's dream and the tone of his reciting it. Joseph also understands that the Pharaoh will need the butler while celebrating his birthday in three days, for which visible preparations were likely underway.

When the chief baker sees that the butler received good news, he also steps forward, hoping for the same. Apparently both the butler and the baker at this time believed that a dream does not reflect the dreaming mind but the nature of the interpreter. With only one possible interpreter present, the baker assumes that only one kind of interpretation is possible. Thus both the butler and the baker refer to their two dreams as one, as "it." Joseph corrects them immediately, referring to their dreams in the plural, because he, as a

model Hebrew psychologist, recognizes that dreams origi-
nate in the dreamer's mind.

Joseph also notes the butler jumps right up to have his
dream interpreted, but the baker hesitates until he receives
a favorable sign, without realizing that the butler's re-assur-
ing interpretation has nothing to do with him. The baker
lives is in a different age, when most folks knew nothing
useful about the nature of dreams or the minds that produced them, leaving this field open to cozening wizards.
The ancient Hebrews recognized that Joseph's own dreams
reflected his angry mind, but they cared more about Joseph's
capacity to reason astutely, leaving psychoanalysis to another age.

Here is Joseph's interpretation of the baker's dream:

> When the chief baker saw that the interpreta-
> tion [of the butler's dream] was good, he said unto
> Joseph, I also was in my dream, and behold, I had
> three white baskets on my head: And in the upper-
> most basket there was of all manner of bake-meats
> for the Pharaoh; and the birds did eat them out of
> the basket upon my head. And Joseph answered
> and said, This is the interpretation thereof: The
> three baskets are three days: Yet within three days
> shall Pharaoh lift up thy head from thee, and shall
> hang thee on a tree; and the birds shall eat thy flesh.

Though Joseph again sounds as if he were a prophet, he
is actually a careful reader of men and their behavior. He
knows that Egypt's Pharaohs frequently suffered sedition,

revolt, and murder. For example, as we turn from Genesis to Exodus, we learn that a new Pharaoh has suddenly arisen, probably because the former Pharaoh was overthrown, a common event in ancient Egypt, accounting for the end of most of the 30 dynasties that governed the country in turn. So when Joseph learns that two of Pharaoh's courtiers are in prison with him, he would naturally look for signs that one or both of them posed a significant threat to Pharaoh.

And, if we recall that the Egyptians believed that birds were divinities, we can read the baker's dream that birds were eating out of his top basket as an expression of fear that his recent behavior would indeed merit Horis's punishment. Joseph might also notice that the baker begins his account of his dream by focusing on himself ("I too was in my dream"), rather than on his service to the Pharaoh, as does the butler, a further hint that the baker might be just the type of man who would join an insurrection against the Pharaoh.

In any case, both of Joseph's well-reasoned interpretations proved correct, not because he was a gifted seer, but because he possessed the kind of reasoning that his rational nation demanded.

II: Joseph Interprets Pharaoh's Dreams

Joseph's capacity to reason is what earns him the opportunity to interpret the dreams of Pharaoh, which allowed him to save Egypt, the Pharaoh, his family, and himself. His story continues in Genesis 41:

> And it came to pass . . . that Pharaoh dreamed; and, behold, he stood by the river. And behold, there came up out of the river seven well favoured kine and fat-fleshed; and they fed in a meadow. And, behold, seven other kine came up after them out of the river, ill favoured and lean-fleshed: and stood by the other kine upon the brink of the river. And the ill-favoured and lean-fleshed kine did eat up the seven well-favoured and fat kine. So Pharaoh awoke. And he slept and dreamed the second time: and dreamed a second time: and, behold, seven ears of corn came up upon one stalk, rank and good. And, behold, seven thin ears and blasted with the east wind sprung up after them. And the seven thin ears devoured the seven rank and full ears. And Pharaoh awoke, it was a dream. . . . and he called for all the magicians in Egypt, and all the wise men thereof: and Pharaoh told him his dream; but there was none that could interpret them unto Pharaoh.

In describing his dreams to all the magicians and wise men of Egypt, Pharaoh treats his dreams as a single dream ("his dream"). What allows the integration of these two dreams (also called "them" in the same sentence) is the capacity to recognize that two dreams by the same mind are likely to share a common theme. Just as the Torah advances psychology by showing that different dreams by different dreamers are products of different minds, it also demonstrates that two, similar dreams produced by a single dreamer's mind during the same night likely reflect self-intensifying preoccupations of that mind. Both Pharaoh and Joseph understand this, but the Pharaoh's understanding is much dimmer than Joseph's. Pharaoh realizes that his double-barreled dreams are ominous, but only Joseph can see exactly what the frightening dreams portend, and what to do about Egypt's approaching famine.

Joseph had asked the butler to remember to speak on his behalf to the Pharaoh when he returned to service, but the butler, not as sharp as a Joseph might like, forgot to do so. Only after the Pharaoh himself suffers troubling dreams that nobody could or would interpret, did the butler recall Joseph's capacities.

When he is telling the Pharaoh about Joseph's insight, the butler, in mid-sentence, suddenly gives up the idea that "we dreamed a dream," and switches to "we dreamed each man according to the interpretation to his dream." This is repeated twice, presumably because it is important for the *Tanach* to be clear about the psychology of dreams:

> Then spoke the chief butler unto Pharaoh, saying, I do remember my faults this day; Pharaoh . . . put me in ward in the captain of the guard's house, both me and the chief baker: and we dreamed a dream [singular] in one night, I and he; we dreamed each man according to the interpretation of his dream. And there was there with us a young man, a Hebrew, servant to the captain of the guard; and

we told him, and he interpreted to us our dreams [plural]; to each man according to his dream he did interpret.

Thus the butler abandons the benighted idea that a single dream can be shared by two dreamers on the same night, and immediately embraces the correct insight that each dream is produced by the mind of an individual dreamer. This itself represents an advance in the science of psychology. But more importantly, the Hebrew reader should note the value placed on Josephs' ability to reason rationally about what he has carefully observed.

That both the Pharaoh and his magicians claimed that they were unable to interpret his two dreams probably means that they *did* recognize what the dreams portended, but didn't know what to do about a devastating famine that would soon overwhelm Egypt. What else could dreams about blasted meat and vegetables augur? It is likely that Pharaoh's magicians didn't want to chance Pharaoh's explosive reaction to bad news, so they claimed ignorance, just like the first messenger to King David, who also was careful not to provoke the wrath of his King on learning that his beloved son, Absalom, was dead.

Like the Pharaoh of the Exodus who asked for a blessing from the Hebrew God as he straddled between his own bird-gods and Hebrew monotheism, this Pharaoh immediately demands that the Hebrew interpreter, and not one of his magicians, be brought to court.

Joseph is cleaned up and delivered to the Pharaoh, who promptly narrates his two terrifying dreams. Because both of these dreams are so coherent, their meaning is obvious: a disastrous famine will soon starve Egypt. What is most needed here is not an interpretation but a higher level of intelligence that can remedy the oncoming disaster.

From the details of Pharaoh's dreams, Joseph sees immediately that Pharaoh is, for good reason, worried about Egypt's vulnerability to famine. A modern reader may not recognize that the Torah has carefully presented a fact of life in the ancient Middle East that would allow any knowledgeable person of that time to recognize immediately what the dreams meant. When Abraham first arrived in the Promised Land, he found much food for thought but no food, forcing him to leave for Egypt almost immediately after planting his tent. Then when famine develops again in Canaan, Jacob has to send his sons to Egypt for food, where they find Joseph in charge of the entire country.

One can still find along the eastern bank of the Nile near modern Cairo an ancient pillar, which marks the height of the Nile as it changes through the seasons; low readings in the spring promised famine. Egypt's ancient name was *Mitzrai-im*, from the Semitic root, *tsar*, narrow. And narrow it is. Modern Egyptians still call their country *Misr*, and modern Hebrew speakers still call Egypt *Mitzrai-im*. Even now, one can see that for long stretches the bone-dry Egyptian desert falls short of the Nile by a mere 18 inches. In Egypt famine is never far away.

Knowing all this, the intelligent Joseph understands that he can interpret Pharaoh's obvious dreams but, more importantly, he knows how to present himself so that he will be given authority to manage the coming famine, as we see in Genesis 41:28-43:

> What God is about to do he sheweth unto Pharaoh. Behold, there come seven years of great plenty throughout all the land of Egypt: And there shall arise after them seven years of famine, and all the plenty shall be forgotten. . . . Now therefore let the Pharaoh look out a man discreet and wise, and set him over the land of Egypt. . . . And Pharaoh said unto Joseph, Forasmuch as God hath shewed thee all this, there is none as discreet and wise as thou art. . . . And Pharaoh said unto Joseph, See, I have set thee over all the land of Egypt. And Pharaoh took off his ring from his hand and put it up Joseph's hand, and arrayed him in vestures of fine linen, and put a gold chain about his neck; and he made him to ride in the second chariot which he had; and they cried be for him, Bow the knee: and he made him ruler over all the land of Egypt.

Again, when Joseph says, "What God is about to do he sheweth unto Pharaoh," he does not likely mean that he received his interpretation directly from God, for if that were so he wouldn't need to hear Pharaoh narrate his dreams. We are likely meant to understand that Joseph possesses the valued Hebrew capacity to reason through the details of what he perceives, and thereby come to a rational conclusion.

But like many of his forefathers, Joseph overreached. Having become lord of Egypt, he took an Egyptian name, married into a pharaonic family, and was embalmed in the Egyptian fashion. Unlike his father, Jacob, whose body was carried back to Israel to be buried with his father, Abraham, Joseph was buried in Egypt:

> So Joseph died . . . and they embalmed him, and he was put in a coffin in Egypt [or "put in a coffin that is Egypt"].

Both in Hebrew and in English, the two nouns in the phrase "in a coffin in Egypt" can be read so that the latter serves as an appositive of the former. In this reading, Joseph is buried in a coffin that *is* Egypt, a place that must be shunned, according to the Torah. Perhaps Joseph's Egyptian mummification is why his name was omitted from the tribes of Israel. In any case, his life remains a memorial to Hebraic reason, and its persistent weakness.

CHAPTER FOURTEEN
PERVERSION

I: THE UNSPEAKABLE

Since the Land was meant to be an emblem of the vision of Abraham, its worth did not lie in its physical size but in its abstract values. Yes, the Hebrews had to conquer Canaan, but they were forbidden to base their nation on mere conquest. They were commanded to remain within strict borders to distinguish ethical monotheism from the immorality of their idolatrous neighbors.

The Hebrews were probably the first nation commanded by their God to refrain from harassing their neighbors, and, more emphatically, from undertaking any expansion of their territory, as explained by Moses in Deuteronomy 2:9-19:

And the Lord said unto me, Distress not the
Moabites, neither contend with them in battle: for
I will not give thee of their land for a possession. .
. . And when thou comest nigh over against the
children of Ammon, distress them not, nor meddle
with them: for I will not give thee of the land of the
children of Ammon any possession.

Despite this prohibition, King David, in his manic days,
undertook the conquest of Moab, thus not only inflating
his already over-blown zeal, but also perverting the Lord's
will.   Here we see again that the ancient Hebrews understood the dangers of excessive augmentation of thought or
action. Especially forbidden was any augmentation of conquest, for excessive militarism perverted the goals of ethical
monotheism.

Just before his forbidden invasion of Moab, David prays
to his Lord at the very end of II Samuel 7:

For thou, O Lord of hosts, God of Israel, hast
revealed to thy servant, saying, I will build thee an
house: Therefore hath thy servant found in his heart
to pray this prayer unto thee . . . . Therefore now
let it please thee to bless the house of thy servant
that it may continued forever before thee.

After this endearing supplication, David marches into
Moab, where he was not supposed to be. But there he was,
in II Samuel 8:1-2:

And after this it came to pass, that David smote the Philistines, and subdued them: . . . And he smote Moab and he measured them with a line, casting them down to the ground: even with two lines measured he to put to death, and with one full line to keep alive. And so the Moabites became David's servants.

David prays fervently and then brazenly perverts God's will, thus reducing the cognitive skills of ethical monotheism to measuring out the dimensions of a killing field. The heroic King David slaughtered two thirds of the Moabite population with arithmetic precision in a place he was not supposed to be.

And this mockery is only part of the *Tanach's* effort to eliminate perverse behavior from their midst. The biblical writers feared that the longstanding Hebrew attraction to idolatry was an intractable perversion of rational thought, and hence they used the starkest of examples to remind themselves of their perverse temptations. That so many forbidden perversions are listed in the *Tanach* must reflect the multiplicity of actual idolatrous practices to which the Hebrews were drawn, including bestiality. This almost unimaginable act would not be forbidden in the Torah if it did not represent an actual temptation which drew the Hebrews away from their God, as we see most succinctly in Exodus 22:18-20:

Thou shall not suffer a witch to live. Whosoever lieth with a beast shall surely be put to death. He that sacrificeth unto any god, save unto the Lord, only, he shall be utterly destroyed.

The forbiddance of bestiality and its connection to the worship of foreign gods, is repeated in Leviticus 18:23 and 20:15-16:

Neither shalt thou lie with any beast to defile thyself wherewith, neither shall any woman stand before a beast to lied down thereto: it is confusion [*tevel*, a perversion, according to Rashi].

And if a man lie with a beast, he shall surely be put to death, and ye shall slay the beast. And if a woman approach to any beast, and lie down thereto, thou shalt kill the woman and the beast.

In Deuteronomy 27:21-26, bestiality is likened to incest and to an even worse taboo, the betrayal of the God of Israel:

Cursed be he that lieth with any manner of beast. . . . cursed be he that lieth with his sister, the daughter of his father, or the daughter of his mother [in ancient Israel a man was permitted four wives, in the manner of Jacob, so that the daughter of his father need not be the daughter of his mother]. . . . Cursed be he that confirmeth not all the words of this law to do them.

Modern readers usually agree that these acts, as well as many (but not all) of the long list of other perversities specified in Leviticus 20, should be discouraged. But these taboo intimacies are not themselves the focus of Leviticus. The ancient Hebrews likely understood these prohibitions as a warning not to metamorphose their intimate relationship with their God into a bestial travesty. Whether or not this intensified warning sufficed is still uncertain for both Jews and gentiles.

CHAPTER FIFTEEN
Sublimation

I: Aristotle's Thoughts about Tragic Theater

Aristotle, along with other ancient Greeks, with their unsur-
passed curiosity, pursued a deep understanding of everything
in heaven and on earth. Archimedes wanted to know why
he could float in water, and Aristotle wanted to know what
motivated intelligent citizens to spend an enjoyable after-
noon watching a tragedy by Sophocles.

As many undergraduates used to know, Aristotle wrote
about this question in his *Poetics*, focusing on the artful
Greek tragedies. Life, as everybody soon learns, is full of
catastrophe, which evokes fear in the yet unharmed, and
pity for those who suffer outrageously right before the eyes
of an attentive audience in a well designed amphitheater.
Aristotle thought that the satisfaction of such a spectacle

derived from what he called *catharsis*, by which he meant something broader than the current medical meaning of the term, which refers to a purgation of disease-bearing fluids, mainly from the gastrointestinal track. What Aristotle had in mind was not a purging of the physical body but of the troubled mind itself, which needed a calming perspective, not an enema.

This idea of art as a way of soothing roiling fears was not far from the modern idea of sublimation, but Aristotle lacked sufficient psychological insight to develop his seminal exploration of how best to manage the overwhelming emotional responses to the mayhem of love and war, leaving psychoanalysis for another age.

II: Freud's Idea of Civilization and its Sublimations

As soon as Freud settled on the idea that every human mind teems with repressed horrors, he found it useful to blame his patients' neuroses on the mind's hodge-podge of desires and fears. His therapy, as we have already noted, depended on moving these denizens of the unconscious into consciousness, where they could be tamed.

But this expensive therapy didn't really take care of the problem. Yes, managing ones most powerful urges was mandatory if one wanted to live in a civilized society, but the necessary suppression of sex and mayhem would inevitably leave many people frustrated by unsatisfied desires. Dr. Freud addressed this problem in his 1930 book, *Civilization and its Discontents*, which also praises civilization's positive qualities.

To adapt to the necessary constraints of civilization, citizens had to find a more acceptable way to discharge their demanding drives. Instead of procreating ad lib, they could improve their lives by creating theater and literature about love and sex. And in place of constant warfare, they could bet on boxing matches, yelling for victory for one gloved gladiator, or the other.

Freud called this elevation of primitive drives *sublimation*, a mental process that tames brutish energies by channeling them into science, sport, innovation, technology, and art. For these arts not only provide distractions from the wild forces of the unconscious mind, they also render civilized life meaningful and pleasurable, at least for most of the people most of the time.

Dr. Freud's daughter, Anna, having escaped from the horrors of Nazi-run Vienna, continued her father's work in London after his death. She focused on the defense mechanisms that patients adopt to manage the frustrations caused by a well-mannered civilization. One of these defense mechanisms was sublimation. One could attend a production of *Oedipus Rex* or *La Traviata* and thereby assuage raging passions by witnessing them played out from the safety of a box seat. This defense would, of course, be of no use in a civilization run by Nazis, even if Hitler liked movies.

One would surmise that this controversial twentieth-century psychology of sublimation, far more sophisticated than Aristotle's idea of catharsis, would not be found in the ancient Hebrew Bible. But, again, to the knowing eye, there it is. By the time Aristotle was writing his Poetics, the Ancient Hebrews were already developing the idea of sublimation. We saw this endeavor in action in the Introduction to this work. The line of Cain turned from fratricide and other primitive drives to a more civilized, sublimated resolve to create useful tools and musical instruments.

III: Blood in the House of the Lord

Here is an example of sublimation that usually escapes our notice because it is so bizarre. First, let us understand that the Children of Israel had as a primary value the sanctity of human life, as represented by blood, thought to be life's essence. Shedding human blood was allowed only in self-defense, and eating any blood was absolutely forbidden, as in Leviticus 7:26-27:

> Moreover ye shall eat no manner of blood, whether it be of fowl or beast, in any of your dwellings. Whatever . . . eateth any manner of blood, even that soul shall be cut off from his people.

This being the case, it is somewhat shocking to find that the dedication of both the altar and Aaron himself in the Temple required a good deal of sprinkled blood, as we see in Exodus 29:20-21:

Then shalt thou kill the ram, and take of his blood, and put it upon the tip of the right ear of Aaron, and on the tip of the right ear of his sons, and upon the thumb of their right hand, and upon the great toe of their right feet, and sprinkle the blood upon the altar round about. And thou shalt take of the blood that is upon the altar, . . . and sprinkle it upon Aaron, and upon his sons, and upon the garments of his sons with him: and he shall be hallowed, and his garments, and his sons, and his sons' garments with him.

This amounts to an expenditure of a lot of blood, the value of which is unclear in a society that sanctifies blood. Likely, the introduction of pagan bloodlust into the holy Temple served as a sublimation of the urge to shed blood, which was thereby dampened.

God Himself proclaims that Cain's urge to shed blood must be restrained, as we see in God's response to Cain's famously snide question:

And the Lord said unto Cain, Where is Abel thy brother? And he said, I know not: Am I my brother's keeper? And He said, What hast thou done? The voice of thy brother's blood crieth out to me from the ground. And now art thou cursed from the earth, which has opened her mouth to receive thy brother's blood from thy mouth.

The Creator adroitly personifies Abel's spilled blood, so that it now has a voice, and so does the earth itself, which is given a mouth to cry out. These harmonizing voices sing out the sanctity of human blood and human life, which Cain has desecrated. Perhaps the creation by his descendants of musical instruments and useful tools atones for his former bestial urges, and so does the story itself, which praises the line of Cain for turning away from violence to wholesome sublimations.

IV: ABRAHAM'S SUBLIMATION OF CHILD SACRIFICE

Other stories in the *Tanach* demonstrate how raw passions might be lifted to a higher level, where they can be mastered. The grandest and most misunderstood of these stories focuses on the binding of Isaac (as it is called in Hebrew), during which the pagan ritual of child sacrifice is circumvented by sublimation.

Many secularists are horrified by God's commanding Abraham to sacrifice his son Isaac, which they deem as primitive as Molech's demand to have children submitted to fire. But the binding of Isaac is told in a Hebraic context; it is meant as a sublime drama that puts an end to the Hebrews' temptation to idolatry, especially their attraction to the cult of child sacrifice, which eventually earned them a tongue-lashing in Jeremiah 19:3-5:

> Thus saith the Lord of hosts, the God of Israel; Behold I will bring evil upon this place … They have … built the high places of Baal to burn their sons with fire for burnt offerings unto Baal.

The ancient and medieval Hebrew commentators discussed the binding of Isaac at length, often disagreeing on details, but generally settling on the idea that this demand placed on Abraham is a kind of test whose necessity is not obvious, since it challenges one of the foundational ideas of Hebraic civilization, which proclaims again and again that human life is sanctified.

In Leviticus 18:21, in Deuteronomy 18:10, and in Ezekiel 23:37, we get this series of prohibitions:

> Thou shalt not let any of thy seed pass through the fire to Molech.
>
> There shall not be found among you anyone that maketh his son or his daughter to pass through the fire.
>
> With their idols have they . . . caused their sons, whom they bare unto me, to pass them through the fire to be devoured.

Abraham must have been familiar with these idolatrous rites, for they were part of the weltanschauung in Ur, from which he had fled. He certainly knew that his hearkening to his immaterial God was distinct from the way pagans communicated with their gods, as exemplified by a carving in about 180 BCE on a pillar in the Temple of Sobek. This all-powerful god possessed the head of a crocodile fitted with human eyes and ears, fixed to an upright body of a man:

The Metropolitan Museum in New York occasionally displays a more accessible version of this crocodile-god, a noble terracotta bust, this time featuring a more careful-ly-crafted human ear to go with its bright eye and its toothy proboscis, fabricated about 150 years before Abraham abandoned Ur:

Now it so happens that this crocodile-god with an ear is in the background of the Hebrew God's contrasting command to listen with a righteous ear, as in Deuteronomy 6:4, for whose translation I substitute a version closer to the Hebrew than that of the King-James translators: "Hear, O Israel: *Adonai*, our God, *Adonai* is one." This famous verse could have been phrased more succinctly, as "Hear, O Israel, Adonai, our God, is One." That the ineffable word for the Hebrew God appears twice is not an equivocation, but a reminder to the ambivalent Hebrews, woven right into their proclamation of their God's uniqueness, that they have often defied Abraham's covenant with duplicity.

Abraham must have been overwhelmingly confused when God, in Genesis 22, commanded him to submit his own son to an act that he knew to be a Hebraic abomination:

> And it came to pass after these things that God did tempt Abraham, and said unto him, Abraham: and he said, Behold, here I am. And he [God] said, Take now thy son, thine only son Isaac, whom thou lovest, and get thee into the land of Moriah: and offer him there for a burnt-offering upon one of the mountains which I will tell thee of. And Abraham rose up early ion the morning . . . and took two of his young men with him, and Isaac his son, and clave the wood for the burnt-offering, and rose up, and went unto the place of which God had told him. . . . And Abraham said unto his young men, Abide ye here, with the ass; and I and the lad will go yonder and worship, and come again to you.

The indication that we are not now in the realm of Molech appears almost immediately. The binding of Isaac is not motivated by the expectations of Abraham's culture, as it would be in the culture of Molech. Rather, there are specific events in the Patriarch's recent past that might be motivating God to tempt Abraham. Just a few verses before the passage above, Abraham made a covenant (*Brit* in Hebrew) with Abimelech, concerning seven goats and seven wells (from which both the ancient and modern city of Beersheba, or Seven Wells, takes its name). *Brit* is the word for the covenant made between Abraham and God, and for male circumcision, the emblem of that covenant. Presumably, it is not a word to be used lightly.

In this context, however, the test of Abraham is in the form of a question, not a command. Are you or are you not in a unique relationship with your God? Or, do you value material things like wells and goats in the same way that you value your relationship with an invisible God and His sacred laws? This is a question asked regularly throughout the *Tanach*, and it is likely in the background here. Pagan sacrifices never involve such questions, nor any questions at all.

There are also two literary allusions here that more emphatically elevate the binding of Isaac above the primitive urge to sacrifice children to a fire god. The first appears in God's ordering Abraham to "get thee into the land of Moriah"; the Hebrew verb here is *lech lecha*, an unusual way of commanding one to get going. It is the same verbal phrase that God used in Genesis 12 to send Abraham on his foundational emigration from Ur to Canaan, where he is to undertake the mission of overcoming idolatry.

A second allusion to Abraham's emigration from Ur to Canaan is the phrase, "offer him there for a burnt-offering upon one of the mountains which I will tell thee of." This echoes the qualifying phrase that God appends to His original order that Abraham should leave his family and birthplace, not to a specific destination, but "unto a land I will shew thee." This vagueness tests Abraham's capacity to understand and accept an abstract idea unsupported by any material specifics. Abraham must abandon the literalism of idolatry in Ur *and* accept the abstract tenets of monotheism, which rest on ideas, on a divinely selected place only in the sense that the place will be valued for its meaning, not its specific location. Abraham had to hold that meaning in his mind as an ideal to pursue, not as a physical destination. Because the Children of Israel persistently failed to hold onto that ideal, they needed and were given the sublime story of the binding of Isaac.

The narrative of this sublimation continues in an elevated way, including humane details that differ sharply from the inhumane nature of child sacrifice. Molech presumably would not care if a father loved his son, nor would he care if the object of sacrifice were an "only child" called "Isaac."

Unsurprisingly, Abraham signals that he does not really want to sacrifice his son; he tells his two servants to wait below Mount Moriah, where the sacrifice is supposed to take place, saying, "I and the lad will go yonder and worship, and we will come again to you." The Hebrew uses the plural "we" to make it clear that Abraham plans to come back down the mountain with his beloved son. Stories about the devotees of Molech presumably do not include details about fathers secretly hoping not go through with the barbaric ritual.

The drama continues to give meaning to a child's life and to life in general. Isaac is perceptive and inquisitive, not at all like an animal or even a toddler to be sacrificed to a merciless god. In the end, God is merciful and Abraham indeed descends the mountain with his son:

> And Abraham took the wood of the burnt offering and laid it upon Isaac his son; and he took the fire in his hand, and a knife: and they went both of them together. And Isaac spake unto Abraham his father: and said, My father: and he said, Here am I, my son. And he said, Behold the fire and the wood: but where is the lamb for a burnt-offering? And Abraham said, My son, God will provide himself a burnt-offering: so they went both of them together.

This repeated comment that Abraham and Isaac "went both of them together" would be of no interest in a pagan ritual. Nor would Abraham's answer to Isaac's pointed question ("where is the lamb?") be mentioned in a rite dedicated to the god Molech. But Abraham's God Himself answers Isaac by providing an appropriate animal for

a burnt-offering, which in the Hebrew world is meant as a sublimated substitute for human sacrifice:

> And they came to the place which God had told him of: and Abraham built an altar there, and laid the wood in order, and bound Isaac his son, and laid him on the altar upon the wood. And Abraham stretched forth his hand, and took the knife to slay his son. And the angel of the Lord called unto him out of heaven, and said, Abraham, Abraham and he said, Here am I. And he [the angel] said, Lay not thine hand upon the lad, neither do thou anything unto him: for now I know that thou fearest [have awe for] God, seeing thou has not withheld they son, thine only son from me. And Abraham lifted up his eyes, and looked, and behold behind him a ram caught in a thicket by his horns: and Abraham went and took the ram, and offered him up for a burn't-offering in the stead of his son.

This last line, both in the original Hebrew and in the English of the King-James translators, emphasizes that this drama is a substitute for, or a sublimation of ("in the stead of"), the usual child sacrifice. And the mountain on which this sublimation is staged is to become the sublime setting of Solomon's Temple.

Since we are *not* here dealing with the usual kind of human sacrifice, the narrative allows the Lord to perform a *deus-ex-machina* rescue, aided by the sudden availability of an appropriate ram that just happened to get its horns stuck in a handy thicket at the right time.

This story is perfectly designed to serve as a sublimation of the inhumane crudity of child sacrifice, and, like all good sublimations, it is meant to mark the end of the actual abomination. In just this way, the world, having discovered the virtues of sublimation, no longer tolerates child sacrifice or boxers killing each other in the ring, at least not often.

Perhaps this test of Abraham can be seen as a punishment for his having just made a casual *Brit* with Abimelech, but the larger idea behind the story of the binding of Isaac is seen in its conclusion:

> And Abraham called the name or that place Jehovah-jireh [God will be seen]: as it is said to this day. In the mount of the Lord it shall be seen. And the angel of the Lord called unto Abraham out of heaven the second time. And said, By myself have I sworn, saith the Lord, because thou has done this thing, and has not withheld thy son, thine only son: . . . I will bless thee, and . . . I will multiply thy seed as the stars of heaven, and as the sand which is on the sea shore: . . . And in thy seed shall all the nations of the earth be blessed: . . . So Abraham returned to his young men, and they rose up and went together to Beersheba.

One may doubt the reality of blessings promised by the Hebrew God, and one may remain horrified by God's imposition of a cruel test on righteous Abraham, but there is little doubt that all nations would be blessed if they banished all forms of child sacrifice, including child labor and child soldiers, substituting for these primitive abuses civilized sublimations.

In a world ordered by righteous sublimations, Beersheba might represent something more sublime than seven wells and seven goats.

V: The Red Heifer as Sublimation.

Of all the mysteries in the Torah, the ritual described in Numbers 19:2-10, commanding the obtaining, sacrificing, and disposing of the remains of a Red Heifer, has remained utterly resistant to interpretation. Neither the Talmudic rabbis, nor Rashi, the doyen of rabbinical interpretation of the *Tanach*, could explain this ritual's complex and seemingly contradictory details. Nor could the learned rabbis agree on the ritual's overarching meaning. In five concise Hebrew words, Rashi concluded, *Ain lecha r'shoot l'harhair acharaycha*, "You do not even have permission to reflect on it."

Here are the opaque verses in the King-James translation, which still sound sufficiently bizarre to explain Rashi's exasperation:

> This is the ordinance of the law which the Lord hath commanded saying, Speak unto the children of Israel, that they bring a red heifer, without spot, wherein is not blemish [without a hint of any color

but red], and upon which never came yoke: And ye shall give it unto Eleazar the priest, that he may bring forth without the camp, and one should slay her before his face: And Eleazar the priest shall take of her blood with his finger, and sprinkle of her blood directly before the tabernacle of the congregation seven times. And one shall burn the heifer in his [Eleazar's] sight; her skin, and her flesh, and her blood, with her dung, shall he burn.

Let us pause here to note that the ancient rabbis, including Rashi, believed that the red color of this ritual cow must be so perfect that not a single spot of another color could be seen in its hide, not even "two black hairs." This extraordinary purity of red has, in fact, never been seen in any cow, not in Israel, and not anywhere else.

The absence for two millennia of any evidence of this creature suggests that further search for its existence would be a wild-goose chase. This imaginary heifer can thrive only as a sublimation in the mind of a pious Jew. The description of the ritual of the red heifer uses poetry to play on the Hebrew linkage of the color red (*adom*) and blood (*dam*), suggesting that this ritual, like the sprinkling of blood on the garments of the High Priest, is meant as a sublimation of the forbidden but all-too common urge to spill human blood.

Like many sublimations, the ritual of the red heifer requires a perceptive audience, which is indeed included in the ritual's description. Notice that Eleazar does not himself sacrifice the animal, but has it done "before his face." Nor does Eleazar burn the heifer; it is done "in his sight." Like those watching ancient Greek Theater, Eleazar is assigned the role of observing a sublime spectacle.

As our passage continues, we learn more about other facets of this poetic drama:

> And the priest shall take cedar wood, and hyssop, and scarlet, and cast it into the midst of the burning heifer.

Now it so happens that cedar wood, hyssop and scarlet are precisely the priestly tools used to cleanse the Israelites' frequent cases of "leprosy," which, as we have seen, is not a physical disease but a mental falling away from Hebrew sanctity, thus requiring a spiritual reckoning.

So too, the red heifer represents not only bloodlust but also a general spiritual failing, requiring a treatment that resembles the treatment of leprosy, which also employs cedar wood, hyssop, and scarlet, as described in Leviticus 14:48-51:

> . . . the priest shall come in . . . . And he shall take to clean the house two birds, and cedar wood, and scarlet, and hyssop: And he shall kill one of the birds in an earthen vessel over running water: and he shall take the cedar wood, and the hyssop, and the scarlet, and the living bird, and dip them in the blood of the slain bird . . . . and sprinkle the house seven times.

That the treatment for "leprosy" and the ritual of the red heifer require the same seven occasions of blood sprinkling, and the same application of cedar wood, scarlet, and hyssop, tells us that they are similar maladies, both involving the management of spiritual decline.

The red heifer is also at one with the use of sprinkled blood to dedicate the House of God. The three rituals together, involving sprinkled blood, scarlet, hyssop, and cedar wood, compose one integrated sublimation, which comprises all that is uplifting and all that is foul in the Hebrew mind, which has the capacity to choose either.

As the description of this ritual continues, we see how difficult it is to emerge unambiguously clean after having dealt with the pure red cow. Because bloodlust is so deeply woven into human character, atonement of any kind, including the ritual of the red heifer, cannot render the penitent permanently pure. Thus, following the burning the red heifer, the priest must wash his clothes and bathe:

> Then the priest shall wash his clothes, and he shall bathe his flesh in water, and afterwards he shall come into the camp, and the priest shall be unclean until the eve. And a man that is clean shall gather up the ashes of the heifer, and lay them up without the camp in a clean place, and it shell be kept for the congregation of the children of Israel for . . . it is a purification of sin.

Of course the rabbis noticed the self-contradicting aspects of a ritual cow that rendered the pure priest impure and then served to make the sinful pure. And why should a clean man be sent to gather up the unclean ashes of the heifer? How might the keeping of the cow's contaminating ashes in a clean place modify contamination? The rabbis had no coherent answers for these questions, perhaps because the idea of sublimation did not yet exist, at least in the minds of the rabbis. But in the Torah, the idea did exist.

The sacrifice of the red heifer, red as red can be, is a sublime way of raising bloodlust to a ritual of the mind. For a purely red cow with absolutely no blemishes, not even two black hairs, does not exist in this world. But there was and is such a thing as persistent bloodlust in the Hebrew (and human) mind, where it confronts more righteous urges. Because bloodlust is a drive that survives in one form or another even after the performance of this sublime rite, it had to be repeated regularly so that the Hebrews might thrive in a humane society.

VI: The Sublime Song of Songs

There is no poem in the Hebrew Bible whose interpretation has been as problematic as that of the Song of Songs. This poem, also known as the Song of Solomon, has defied every attempt to find the right key to unlock its enigma. The song's focus on intensely passionate love made many ancient rabbis think it inappropriate for canonization. On the other hand, Rabbi Akiva believed not only that the Song of Songs should be included in the *Tanach* but that it, by itself, would suffice to govern the world justly, had the Torah not been given on Mount Sinai.

So it came to be that most interpretations of the poem, be they by Jews, Christians, or agnostic literary scholars, start with the assumption that it is an allegory of one kind or another, especially an allegory about the importance of matrimony, or about God's frustrated love for his stubborn people, or the people's unreliable love for their God.

But the idea that Song of Songs was an allegory didn't quite explain all its details, especially its most erotic aspects. Sexual yearning didn't seem a proper way to allegorize either marriage, or man's love for God, or God's love for man. For hundreds of years rabbinic interpreters failed to make The Song of Songs fit any of their allegorical schemes.

One obvious problem was the well-known fact that idolatry was characterized, under the sex goddess, Ashtoreth, by just this kind of intense lust. In the ancient Levant, prostitutes were hired to lure men to attend idolatrous services, again and again. These enticing ladies were all called in Hebrew *Kedisha*, which comes from the root of the Hebrew word for holy, *Kadosh*, as in Leviticus 19:2: "Ye shall be holy: for I the Lord your God am holy." At the root of the rabbis' problem with the Song of Songs was its seeming linkage of canonized Hebrew poetry to a hyper-sexualized idolatrous practice.

Ibn Ezra, known as a realist who wrote an entire book on the Song of Songs, gave up viewing the entire poem as a well-designed allegory. He separated the frankly erotic verses into their own section, which required a different kind of interpretation. He did not make clear what connection the erotic section might have with the allegorical section, but he came very close to distinguishing how allegory differs from sublimation.

What, then, is an allegory, and what is a sublime text? Allegorical stories appear throughout classical literature, such as in Plato's famous Allegory of the Cave in *The Republic*, and even in the Hebrew Bible, as in Psalm 80's allegory of the Vine. An allegory tells a coherent story where all the details fit together on two different levels; the surface level makes its own sense, and so does the deeper level, whose meaning enriches the surface level.

As an example, consider a few verses of Psalm 80:

> Turn us again, O God of hosts . . . Thou has brought a vine out of Egypt: thou has cast out the heathen, and planted it. Thou preparedst room before it, and caused it to take deep, and it filled the land. The hills were covered with the shadow of it, and the boughs thereof were like the goodly cedars. She sends out her boughs unto the sea, and her branches unto the river.

The story of the vine spreading widely from Mediterranean Sea to the Jordan river is easily recognized as the story of the Children of Israel spreading across the Land that they were promised. The allegory brings to the foreground the fecundity of the Land and thus focuses attention on the issue that most needs attention: the new residents' responsibility to cultivate the Land, and not abuse the ethics for which it stands:

> Why hast thou then broken down her hedges, so that all they which pass by the way do pluck her [i.e., steal her fruits]? The boar out of the wood doth waste it, and the wild beast of the field doth devour it. Return, we beseech thee, O God of hosts: look down from heaven and behold, and visit this vine: . . . It is burned with fire, it is cut down: they perish at the rebuke of thy countenance. . . . So we will not go back from thee: quicken us, and we will call on thy name.

The allegory here does what allegories are supposed to do, which is to clarify what matters. That which might be superficially regarded when delivered via direct language becomes more meaningful in a well-constructed allegory. What matters is not the vine, not the fire, not even the Land, but the otherwise easily-ignored fact that the Children of Israel have behaved like wild beasts of the field, showing no regard for the sacred meaning of the gift they have been given. The allegory of Psalm 80 needs to have that emphasized so that the Hebrews might yet again "call on Thy name."

One need not accept the message of an allegory to understand that allegory works differently from sublimation.

There is no obvious message on the surface of sublimations. Sublimations actually work to obscure what they try to elevate. He who screams with delight when his favorite boxer knocks out his opponent need not be aware of why he is screaming; in fact, he does not want to acknowledge his homicidal drives, now being managed by the unconscious brute on the ring's mat. Those who enjoy the sublime beauty of The Song of Songs may not agree that it is a Freudian sublimation, but they might concur that a long line of Hebrew commentators failed to find a satisfactory interpretation for this much-admired poem because they did not recognize the genre of sublimation.

Ibn Ezra made it only halfway to the truth about the Song of Songs, probably because Freud's ideas about sublimation were not yet available. Since the literary use of allegory was well established in the era of the Hebrew Bible, it became the most-used genre in which to express a complex emblematic story. That the mind might also have a capacity to elevate the intense desire for sexual gratification into the realm of the sublime was not yet recognized, nor was the possibility that the mind could sublimate other intense and complex drives.

Nevertheless, the writer of the Song of Songs knew much about how to channel intense passion into ethereal poetry; a glance reveals its sublimity. Let us look at Chapter 2:4-6, from which the censorious translators removed frankly erotic innuendos of the lady's longing for sexual love from her lover.

He brought me to the banqueting house [house of wine], and his banner over me was love [and he hoisted his flag over me with love]. Stay with me with flagons [flasks of wine], comfort me with apples: for I am sick of love. His left hand is under my head, and his right hand doth embrace me.

In the Hebrew, the word translated here as "his banner" is *deeglo*, "his flag," which, in this context, has obvious sexual connotations. What is hoisted over this intoxicated lady is her physical lover, his left hand under her head, and his right hand embracing her, with the anatomical details suggesting that his member is also hoisted (the adjectival form of *degel* is *deegool*, "prominent"). If King Solomon, the lover of the Queen of Sheba, is indeed the author of this poem, about what besides the art of sex is he singing? Certainly Ibn Ezra would confine these verses to his frankly erotic section of the poem.

The lady here continues in the same erotic vein, and her lover responds with more of the same, as Chapter 4 slides into Chapter 5:

Awake, O north wind: and come, thou south: blow upon my garden that, that the spices thereof may flow out. Let my beloved come into his garden, and eat his pleasant fruits. [And the lover responds,]I am come into my garden, my sister, my spouse: I have gathered my myrrh with my spice: I have eaten my honeycomb with my honey: I have drunk my wine with my milk.

Of course the lady responds to her lover's allusive language:

> I sleep, but my heart waketh: it is the voice of my beloved that knocketh, saying open to me, my sister, my love, my dove, my undefiled: for my head is filled with dew, and my locks with the drops of the night.

To which the lover unsurprisingly responds with intensification of his passion, and so does his beloved:

> I have put off my coat: how shall I put it on? I have washed my feet: how shall I defile them? [And she responds,] My beloved put in his hand by the hole in the door [Hebrew *chor*, aperture], and my bowels were moved for him.

Perhaps this lady "sick of love" represents the many strange women who lured the Hebrews away from their Lord, and perhaps her lover represents those misled Hebrews who, like Solomon, were easily charmed by their own Queens of Sheba with open apertures?

Only the sublime nature of the poetry compensates for the dangerous drives that are herein thinly masked and thereby managed, as we see in 8:5-7:

> Who is this that cometh up from the wilderness, leaning upon her beloved? . . . Set me a seal upon thine heart, as a seal upon thine arm: for love is a strong as death: jealousy is cruel as the grave:

the coals thereof are coals of fire, which hath a most vehement flame. Many waters cannot quench love, neither can the flood drown it: if a man would give all the substance of his house for love, it would be utterly contemned.

This last line is rarely quoted and even less often remembered, so successful be this sublimation of that which should be "utterly contemned." Without this lovely poetry, the ancient Hebrews would not be fit to overcome the dangers that ensnared even the wise King Solomon, with his 300 concubines and the tantalizing Queen of Sheba. And so the Children of Israel were offered the Song of Songs as a sublimation of the powerful urges that drew them away from higher aspirations. Its music elevates destructive human passions into a realm where a libidinous people might survive "the flood."

VII: The Sublimation of Amalekite Violence

Let us go back to the Amalekites, that mysterious, violent people who find a thematic place throughout the *Tanach*, with one thread of their story appearing here and there and everywhere, in Genesis 14:7, Genesis 36, Exodus 17:8-16, Numbers 13:29, Numbers 14:45, Numbers 24:20 (Baalam), Deuteronomy 25:17-19, Judges 3:13, Judges 6:3, I Samuel 15:2, I Samuel 30 (David), I Chronicles 4:42, Psalm 83:7, and the Book of Esther. Certainly, the literary editors of the *Tanach* would not have repetitively focused their readers' minds on these desert wanderers if they did not wish to elevate and thereby manage the miserable Hebrew temptations to mimic the Amalekites.

When all the threads of the Amalekite story are woven together in the reader's mind, a tapestry on the nature of motiveless hate and irrational violence slowly emerges, an artful display meant for the attention of those Hebrews with their own mindless tendencies, like Korach, Samson, David, and Solomon, as well as underachievers like Lot and Lady Lot, Noah and Manoah, King Saul, and like Zimri with his Midianite concubine Cozbi. But once seen in its full, sublime panorama, the significance of the Amalekites lies not primarily in their motiveless hatred of the ancient Hebrews, but in their primitive rebellion against the Hebrew God.

Yes, the brutish Amalekites attacked the weakest stragglers of the recently-liberated slaves, but this scheme was actually more stupid than harmful, for their fragile targets were not likely to be carrying anything of value, nor would their death undermine the Hebrews' military might. The Amalekites main interest was not in killing warriors or capturing booty but in rejecting the monotheist vision of these invaders. They earned their prominent role in the *Tanach* not merely as a foolish and brutish people, but as a warning to the Hebrews that their own repetitive rejection of the God of Abraham made them appear as foolish and brutish as the Amalekites.

The spies who couldn't perceive the virtues the Holy Land disobeyed Moses and stupidly made a second assault on Canaan. They immediately were felled by the former-ly-defeated Amalekites, as we saw earlier, in Number 14: 41-45.

> And Moses said, Wherefore do ye transgress the commandment of the Lord? But it shall not prosper. Go not up, for the Lord is not among you; that ye not be smitten before your enemies. For the Amalekites and the Canaanites are there before your, and ye shall fall by the sword . . . . But they presumed to go up . . . . Then the Amalekites came down and smote them.

Similarly, legions of other Hebrew dullards turned their faces away from the commands of their Lord, including those who wished to stone Moses and Aaron for refusing to take them back to Egypt.

The ancient rabbis rather simplistically branded the Amalekites as exhibiting motiveless hatred, but David, in Psalm 83, sees more deeply. The Amalekites were part of a league of nations that cared more about rejecting the Hebrew God than killing a few thirsty stragglers in the hot desert, as we see in Psalm 83:

> Keep not thou silence, O God, hold not thy peace, and be not still, O God. For, lo, thine ene-mies make a tumult, and they that hate thee . . . have taken crafty counsel against thy people, and consulted against thy hidden ones [against those sheltered by thee]. They have said, Come, and let us

cut them off from being a nation, that the name of Israel be not in remembrance. For they [the ungodly confederacy] have consulted with [each other and came to] one consent: they are confederate against thee.

David understands that the Amalekites and their confederacy assaulted the Hebrews not simply because they were foreigners, but because their monotheistic views undermined idolatrous belief in multiple gods. The Amalekites are given so much attention in the *Tanach* because the Hebrew themselves often chose the customs of the Amalekite confederacy, who were "against thee," i.e., the Hebrew God.

So just as the Amalekites wished that "the name of Israel be not in remembrance," the Hebrew God commands His stubborn Children of Israel to obliterate the name of Amalek, but in a sublime way. The Hebrews, as a mindful people, must *not forget to obliterate* the name of Amalek so that this people might serve as a permanent reminder of the ubiquitous wish to destroy the idea of monotheism. The ancient rabbis realized that the Amalekite league was larger and longer-lasting than the paltry union described in the *Tanach*. Only the yearly ritual of enacting this sublime commandment during the annual cycle of Torah readings might provide an antidote to the Hebrew temptation to imitate the Amalekites and the other nations in their blasphemous League.

In many synagogues around the world, the verses below from Deuteronomy 25:19 are read once from the Torah and then repeated to a standing congregation:

> Therefore it shall be, when the Lord thy God hath given the rest from all thine enemies round about . . . . that thou shall blot out the remembrance of Amalek from under heaven; thou shalt not forget it.

The mental gymnastics required by this command to remember to blot out the remembrance of the Amalekite story, together with many similar threads, weave a complex tapestry that distinguishes the vision of the ancient Hebrews from that of any other people.

Even the Book of Esther, read annually in the synagogue on the holiday of Purim, partakes in the Amalekite tapestry. The Book's arch-villain is Haman, a descendant of Agag, King of the Amalekites, whom Samuel ordered Saul to kill, not for revenge but to see if Saul possessed the faculties to be a monotheistic King. In the Book of Esther, Haman despises Mordechai precisely because the Jew refuses to bow down to him, thus threatening his belief in his own idolatrous gods.

As we view this complex weave of the Amalekite story, we find ourselves in a sublime narrative, focused on the pagan's violent rejection of monotheism, as well as on the Hebrew temptation to imitate the Amalekites and thereby escape the burdensome commandments of their unseen

God. This unresolvable psychological conflict renders the Hebrews a people that "shall dwell alone," according to Balaam in Numbers 23:9.

It was Balaam, we recall, who lifted the Hebraic ambivalence into the sublime, where it meets the many fragments of the story of the despised Amalekites. In that sublime realm, the Hebrews might come to understand in an oblique way that they were often as contemptuous of themselves as the Amalekites were of the Hebrew God.

VIII: The Sublimity of Hebrew Dietary Laws

The *Tanach*'s dietary laws have long been recognized as separating the ancient Hebrews and their descendants from other nations. In her 1966 book, appropriately titled *Purity and Danger*, Mary Douglas suggested that the chief function of the Hebrew dietary laws was to separate the Hebrews from the idolatrous nations that would perpetually threaten them. If people do not break bread together they are, literally, less companionable, thus less likely to share cultural habits. Culinary separation helps the Hebrews avoid the foreign beliefs that undermine the life-sustaining values of ethical monotheism. Because the Children of Israel found that their dietary laws did not satisfactorily protect them from mimicking their idolatrous neighbors, the ancient and medieval rabbis added, through the centuries, more and more dietary regulations.

The original dietary rules mainly focused on the commandment to distinguish those kosher animals from those that were forbidden. The land animals that could be slaughtered for meat were those with cloven hooves and chewed cud; the others were *tref*. Kosher fish are those with fins and scales; shrimp and lobster are *tref*.

The rabbis of the Talmud thought these important distinctions so easy to ignore that they proclaimed new rules, following their commitment to protect important principles by placing "fences" around vulnerable laws.

The new rules included a detailed description of proper kosher slaughter, as well as strict rules about maintaining separate sets of crockery and utensils, one set for meat dishes and a second set for milk dishes. All of these new prescriptions provided opportunities for the Hebrews to practice dietary distinctions so that they might sharpen their capacity to distinguish the righteous laws of monotheism from the many forms of idolatry.

Nevertheless, even the modern imposition of the necessity to wash meat china and milk china in separate dishwashers has failed to provide a satisfactory explanation for the foundational verse in the Torah that provides the basis of separating milk-products from meat products: "Do not seethe a kid in its mother's milk."

If we pay close attention to two-millennia of rabbinic discussion of this peculiar prohibition of a culinary act that would not in any case occur often, we can come to a clearer understanding of the need for kosher practice.

The way the Torah crafts the command to abolish kid-seething elevates this prohibition into poetry, and thereby into the realm of sublimation. A brief, condensed phrase, something like a haiku, thrice repeated, gives the commandment a chiming significance. Here are all three, each in its own signifying context:

> The first of the first fruits of thy land thou shalt bring into the house of the Lord, thy God. **Thou shalt not seethe a kid in its mother's milk.**
>
> —Exodus 23:19

> Thou shalt not offer the blood of my sacrifice with leaven; neither shall the sacrifice of the feast of Passover be left unto the morning. The first of the first fruits of thy land thou shalt bring into the house of the Lord, thy God. **Thou shalt not seethe a kid in its mother's milk.** And the Lord said unto Moses, Write thou these words: for after the tenor of these words I have made a covenant with thee and with Israel.
>
> —Exodus 34:25-27

> Thou shalt not eat of any thing that dieth of itself: thou shalt give it unto a stranger that is in thy gates, that he may eat it . . . for thou art a holy people unto the Lord, thy God. **Thou shalt not seethe a kid in its mother's milk.**
>
> —Deuteronomy14:21

In this emblematic realm, the commandment not to seethe a kid in its mother's milk is meant as another reminder to the Hebrews not to be brutish, and, by extension, not to participate in any abomination. Cooking a kid in its mother's milk will disturb neither the oblivious goat nor her kid, but the humane chef, if he be a Hebrew, will note, from the three varying contexts of this sublime culinary command, how the brutishness of the act would separate him from the holiness of the Abrahamic Covenant.

In its first appearance, the prohibition against kid-seething is linked to an emblem of that Covenant, the Land of Israel. Every year, the first fruits of that Land must be consecrated to the Hebrew God. In its second appearance, our puzzling prohibition becomes less puzzling when we see that it is connected to the meaning of "Passover," which is mentioned to remind the Hebrew of his liberation from the brutality and the folly of idolatry. And in its third appearance, the prohibition is linked to another prohibition of its kind, that against eating road-kill, which is also animalistic and not fit for the Hebrew who must distinguish himself from the brutish idolater.

Though most rabbinic interpretations of this commandment focus on the literalness of separating milk products from meat, other esteemed commentators interpret the thrice-promulgated command in a more sublime way. In his much-admired *Guide for the Perplexed*, 3:48, Maimonides recognizes the inhumanity of kid-seething, and thus its prohibition serves as a reminder to shun the inhumane acts of idolaters. A similar interpretation is give by Rashbam, the Twelfth-century grandson of Rashi, and by another revered scholar of the Twelfth century, Ibn Ezra, who seems embarrassed by his challenge to the common rabbinic belief that there are commandments in the Torah that cannot be understood beyond the fact that they must be obeyed simply because they are the Word of God:

> We have no need to seek the reason that it is prohibited, for this is hidden even from those of understanding. But perhaps God commanded us not to do it because it demonstrates a certain cruelty.

Ibn Ezra acknowledges the established rabbinic opinion that there is no reason to seek an explanation for why seething a kid in its mother's milk is forbidden, and then he gives an explanation. The act is forbidden because it is cruel, and cruelty, a form of sadomasochism, is inconsistent with monotheistic holiness.

Ibn Ezra is careful about slipping in his interpretation of kid-seething because of the way ancient rabbis and their followers had divided the Torah's commandments into three categories, whose names in Hebrew are distinct kinds of divine law. In English, the multiple words used to translate these three categories, such as *judgment, law, ordinance, regulation*, and *decree* are all ambiguous synonyms.

The rabbinic category *Mishpatim*, or Judgments, contains the Torah's rational laws that resemble secular laws legislated by any intelligent assembly of men, such as those forbidding murder and theft.

The category *Aidot*, or Testimonials, contains laws that are understandable in human terms but refer to rituals and observances that would not likely occur to human beings if they were not commanded by the Torah, such as keeping the Sabbath or observing Passover. They are called Testimonials because they corroborate the value of the observances commanded.

The third category, *Chukim*, is the one that worried Ibn Ezra and concerns us here. It contains laws that derive from the understanding of God Himself and would be unlikely to occur to human beings, such a the command to observe the ritual of the Red Heffer, and the command not to wear a coat made of a mixture of materials from distinct species (*Shatnez*). The Torah even forbids planting an orchard with mixed trees, a commandment that mortal men find baffling.

Rashi and other medieval scholars, failed to find a good explanation in human terms for this third category of laws. Part of the reason for this inability to interpret, beyond the belief that God wants the Hebrews to follow his commands even if they don't understand them, is the failure of the rabbis to recognize the concept of sublimation and the literary genre that makes use of it.

In the deepest sense, the dietary laws given to the Hebrews are not arbitrary commands designed to challenge the wobbly Hebrews' capacity to obey their Lord, but as sublime exercises designed to render the Children of Israel capable of distinguishing justice from injustice and divine creativity from idolatrous fabrications.

Here are the words of Rashi that pertain to those dietary *Chukim* (ordinances) that forbid consuming foods that most people find nutritious. Leviticus 18:4-5 gives general statements about the kind of laws that God calls "my ordinances," or, in Hebrew, *Chukati*, on which Rashi's following commentary is focused:

> You shall do my judgments and keep my ordinances [*Chukati*] to walk therein: I am the Lord your God. Ye shall therefore keep my statutes [*Chukati*] and my judgments: which if a man do, he shall live in them: I am the Lord.

Rashi understands that this class of divine law includes the prohibition against eating pork, and he notes that other nations without the Torah will of course see no reason to follow a law that forbids healthy food for no good reason. But framed between two verses that proclaim that the Legislator is "the Lord your God," the prohibition against eating pork becomes a sublime act that distinguishes those who choose monotheism from those who do not.

Here is how Rashi summarizes the function of that class of laws that forbid the mixture of wool and linen, and the eating of pork:

These are matters concerning which the evil inclination reacts by asking why should we observe them, and the non-Jewish nations of the world likewise react concerning them; for example, the prohibition against eating pork . . . . Therefore it [the Torah] says, "I am HaShem [*The Name*, a humble Hebrew substitution for the ineffable name of their God], which implies, My decree is upon you, you are not permitted to be exempt from it.

Perhaps it is not surprising that Rashi, the most esteemed of Hebrew commentators, comes even closer than Ibn Ezra to recognizing the sublime nature of Judaic dietary laws, whose function is to distinguish the Children of Israel from "non-Jewish nations of the world," and from those recalcitrant Hebrews who follow their own "evil inclination," which is the rabbinic term for the dangerous forces in the mind that can and do drive kings and giant slayers into cruelty and brutishness, like those who would seethe a kid in its mother's milk, even those like David and Solomon.

In his commentary to Leviticus 18:4-5, Rashi mentions other *Chukim* that can also be categorized as sublimations that distinguish monotheists from idolaters. The law forbidding the wearing of a coat woven with mixed threads is in the same category as the commandment forbidding the eating of pork, but Rashi could not quite see that these laws are sublimations of the longstanding Hebrew struggle to distinguish the God of Abraham from the idolatrous gods worshipped by the likes of Delilah and the Queen of Sheba.

In this perspective, the Torah forbids planting a mixture of trees in a single orchard. For one kind of tree is distinct from another kind of tree, just as a wool thread is distinct from a linen thread, and a righteous honoring of life is distinct from human sacrifice. All of these distinctions are sublimated rituals to help the Hebrews distinguish their invisible God from a god carved from a burnt log.

Those who miss the poetry of these sublimations guess that the forbiddance of eating of pork is meant as a health alert. If the prohibition against eating safe and nutritious food is not for health reasons, it makes no sense at all, say modern literalists. To support their argument that pork *must be* unhealthy, they cite the fact that wild boars in Mongolia occasionally carry *Trichinella*, the parasite that causes trichinosis. Of course, they are correct about this factoid, as we can learn from a case study in the *New England Journal of Medicine* from October 4, 2018. An American man who attended a barbeque of wild boar in Mongolia indeed came home with trichinosis.

But this would not be of interest to Rabbi Ishmael, who, we recall, believed that the Torah was written in the language of men. He didn't know what idiolect of the language of men the Hebrew God might have had in mind, but he probably would have doubted that it was the language of the *New England Journal of Medicine*. Perhaps he would be more likely to accept that *Chukim* are sublimations, like David's Psalms, Solomon's Song of Songs, and Jeremiah's Lamentations.

In any case, the Torah is not primarily interested in medical lore or any other form of literalist thinking, as we have seen. Rather, the important idea behind declining pork, and separating cud chewers from those animals that don't, is the idea of *separation* itself. Jews make distinctions between animals mainly because the ritualized practice of distinction-making is a sublime way of combatting the Hebrews' persistent difficulty in distinguishing monotheism from idolatrous folly.

The capacity to distinguish, *LeHavdil* in Hebrew, is at the root of Judaism. The Hebrew God created the world via a series of distinctions, such as light from darkness, as described in Genesis 1; the Sabbath and other holy days are sharply distinguished from other days; and a Jew is distinguished from a gentile by circumcision and adherence to Mosaic Law, which includes the distinction between nutrition that enhances one's respect for life and food that is mere sustenance.

In the same verse in Deuteronomy that prohibits the seething of a kid in its mother's milk, the Torah also prohibits the eating of road kill:

> Thou shalt not eat of any thing that dies of itself: thou shalt give it unto a stranger that is in thy gates . . . or thou may sell it unto an alien, for thou are an holy people unto the Lord thy God.

This, too, is often misread as a medical solution to a health problem, for is not a dead animal likely rotting, infested with disease-bearing maggots? But the Torah allows the selling of these carcasses to non-Jews, which would not be the case if road-kill truly caused disease. For, as we have seen, the Torah forbids treating the stranger unjustly; thus the selling of disease-carrying carrion to strangers would not be allowed if the carrion were forbidden for health reasons. That it *is* allowed derives from the fact that a stranger can have no interest in the Hebrew meaning of this commandment, which is meant to remind the Hebrews to avoid idolatry and all its disgusting aspects.

Even those who do not recognize the existence of holiness might agree that it is no accident that the same phyla of animals that the Hebrews excluded from their diet are exactly those that idiomatic English uses to counter brutishness. When a companion acts avariciously, we say, "Don't be a pig." And when a lawyer friend chases ambulances, we admonish him with, "Don't be a bottom-feeder."

Similarly, when the Torah insists that a Jew should avoid "unclean" food, the reason is not because the food is medically dangerous, not simply because God forbids it, but because it represents everything unsanctified. When taken literally, the Jewish dietary laws may appear foolish, but they actually serve as a sublime way to reign in human brutishness.

In contrast, in the West new dietary fads spring up now and again to dictate what people should eat, usually under the literalist mantra that proclaims, "You are what you eat." But in the Torah's view, Jews would do well by choosing food that provides both nutrition *and* a reminder to lead a sacred, creative, and meaningful life, so that they remain who they were always meant to be.

Perhaps Rashi would have agreed with this formulation if he had recognized the *Tanach*'s use of the literary genre of sublimation. He might then have categorized *Chukim* as sublimations, still divine commandments, but ones that elevate daily acts into the sublime distinction between Judaic monotheism and the secular self-satisfaction of becoming what you just ate.

Since Rashi seems to have agreed with the essentials of this interpretation of *Chukim*, he might have sought a Hebrew word for the idea of sublimation, probably borrowing one that he already knew. In commenting on the Song of Songs 5:10, which hints at the lady's sexual pleasure, Rashi is puzzled by the word *dagool*, which he takes to mean *prominent, elevated in strength,* like *soldiers,* related to the prominent flags of the camping Tribes of Israel, as described in Ezekiel 16:7.

As we have seen, the meaning of *dagool* in the Song of Songs refers to the male sex organ, but there is another meaning of *dagool* (*dagoolim* in the plural) that might have served Rashi well in the Eleventh century as an appropriate characterization of *Chukim*. In his Twentieth-century Hebrew dictionary, Avraham Even-Shushan gives the meaning of *Chukim* as "The raising of an object to a symbol or an ideal," which happens to be a good definition of *sublimation.*

Of course, there are many other Hebrew words to express the central idea of ethical monotheism, which is the elevation of thought and behavior into the realm of Judaic understanding. *Dagool* is not prominent among those words, perhaps because it is not euphonious, and perhaps because there are other words for elevation, like those used in commands for animal sacrifice, which focus on material acts, while *Chukim*, or, if you will, *Dagoolim*, focus on poetic or mental acts with no material object present, such as reading Lamentations on the Fast Day of the Ninth of Av, or refraining from work on the Sabbath to acknowledge God's completion of His work of Creation. This bifurcation of sublimation into two types probably prevented Hebrew scholars from perceiving their unity.

Unlike the words to describe sublime activities that are *not* performed on physical objects, the Hebrew words that refer to sublime acts that *are* performed on material object derive from the root *Oleh*, the word for going up to the Land, an emblematic exercise performed in a material place. Similarly, an *Olah*, an offering brought up to Jerusalem to be ritually burnt, lifted the material animal out of its ancient role in idolatrous practice into the spiritual realm of the Hebrew God, where the going up of smoke signaled devotion to the unique Creator of human dignity.

We can appreciate how material underpinnings are elevated into a sublime activity in the ancient Hebrew rituals of animal sacrifice, including the one that is to be performed yearly on the first day of the new year, as commanded in Numbers 29:1-2:

> Thus on the seventh month, on the first day of the month, ye shall have a holy convocation: . . . And ye shall offer a burnt offering for a sweet savor unto the Lord; one young bullock, one ram, and seven lambs of the first year without blemish.

Because the performance of this ritual is commanded in the ethereal realm of sublimation, the bullock, the ram, and the lambs have shed their material nature (even in their material state they must be without blemish) to become metaphoric. The smoke of these animals does not literally satisfy the olfactory pleasure of the Lord. A literal reading here is of course ridiculous, as there is no such thing as a divine nose. What is expressed in Numbers 29 is a metaphor for the sublime meeting of minds between the Children of Israel and their Lord. The sacrificial ritual honors a hopeful reconciliation between their righteous God and the Hebrews' less-than-righteous behavior during the previous year.

Thus, an *Olah*, a burnt offering, rises above the pagan's material gift to a material god, to become a sublime expression of devotion. On the other hand, the Hebrews were also commanded to celebrate rituals that involved no material object at all. These acts, which we might place in the category of *Dagoolim*, are poetic tributes to Judaic holiness, sublimations of the mental capacities that might offset brutish drives that are foreign to ethical monotheism.

IX: Lamentations as Elegy:
A sublime mourning

Those who canonized the Book of Lamentations appropriately classified it as poetry, as indeed it is. The book is not a history of the destruction of Jerusalem, like that found in the Book of Kings, not a book of reproach, like Jeremiah's Prophecy, not even a description of Hebrew mourning, but an elegy, composed by the poet Jeremiah himself.

The elegy is a classical genre, a poetic way of reckoning with loss, especially the death of an admired or beloved soul-mate. Echoes of this genre appear many times in the *Tanach*, which uses its own form of versification and rhyme. In ancient Hebrew poetry, each line is broken into two parts, one longer than the other. The lines rhyme not by sound but by chiming ideas, as in these verses, cited by Sir William R Nicoll in his *Bible Commentary*:

> Keep thy tongue from evil/
>   And thy lips from speaking guile.
> Depart from evil and do good/
>   Seek peace and produce it.
>   Psalm 34:13-14

The virgin of Israel is fallen/
  She shall no more rise.
She is forsaken upon her land/
  There is none to raise her up.
                                    —Amos 5:2

Remembering mine afflictions and my
misery/
  The wormwood and the gall,
My soul hath them still in remembrance/
  And is humbled in me.
This I recall in my mind/
  Therefore I have hope.
                          —Lamentations 3:20-21

It is of the LORD's mercies that we are
not consumed/
  Because his compassions fail not/
They are new every morning/
  Great is thy faithfulness.
                          —Lamentations 3:22-23

Poets continued to write elegies from antiquity into the
Nineteenth century and beyond. Perhaps students of English literature still recall Thomas Gray's "Elegy written in a
Country Churchyard, " which owes much to Lamentations
in that it mourns a terrifying loss:

  The boast of heraldry, the pomp of pow'r,
  And all that beauty, all that wealth e'er gave,

Awaits alike th' inevitable hour.
The paths of glory lead us but to the grave.

The morbid thoughts here follow the same theme as Lamentations, but Gray lifts this dreary loss into the realm of Christian sublimation. His poem includes the death of the poet Milton and the destruction inflicted by the regicidal Cromwell, but the conclusion of his elegy serves as an antidote for the terrifying loss that awaits all men:

THE EPITAPH

No farther seek his merits to disclose,
Or draw his frailties from their dread abode,
(There they alike in trembling hope repose)
The bosom of his Father and his God.

By raising the fate of all men into the sublimity of Christian faith, Gray overcomes his fear of the grave, his own "dread abode."

The Book of Lamentations similarly becomes less mournful and more celebratory, but of course in a distinctively Judaic vein. What the poetry of Lamentations elevates is the Hebrews' capacity to draw on their own monotheistic mindfulness to lift them out of the misery they had created for themselves. Because Jeremiah can "recall" in his mind the details of his suffering and then weave them into an elegy, he can suggest that the Hebrews might yet apply their creativity to mitigate their plight.

In this vein Jeremiah turns to the language of rational examination, to the diction of science and philosophy, thus abandoning mere moaning. Suddenly, in Lamentations 3:39-40, we are in the Hebrew House of Study, where the Hebrews can examine their troubled minds:

> Wherefore doth a living man complain for [i.e., about] the punishment of his sins? Let us [instead] search and try [*Nachkor* = investigate] our ways again unto the LORD. Let us lift up our heart [mind] with our hands unto God in the heavens.

Again, we can read the "heart and "hands" as metaphoric for the complete human being, capable of probing his or her mind. As a poem, the Book of Lamentations is not a dirge but a sublimation composed particularly for the Hebrews, who needed to re-apply their sanctified creativity. Thus the *Tanach* insists that adherence to ethical monotheism rests on both an understanding of the creative mind and on a well-honed capacity to interpret artful narrative.

EPILOGUE
Bible, Literacy, and Mind

Because the ancient Hebrews bequeathed to their children the obligation to live according to their Torah, they, more than other people, became known as the People of the Book. The Greeks often quoted Homer, but they, unlike the Hebrews, were not guided by any one book or by any one god. Plato did acknowledge that the gods must be honored, but he found it necessary to invent his own books of instruction, and these, *The Republic* and *The Laws*, were written in the spirit of an ongoing Socratic discussion. The precise formula for an ideal set of Greek laws was never discovered, and never legislated.

In *The Laws*, the main character, called the Athenian (probably a stand-in for Plato himself) converses with two others, one from Sparta and one from Crete, who bring different perspectives from their cities of origin to the question of how to create the most just society by legislating wise-ly. Nothing was decided, the three perspectives were not integrated into a single unity, and no laws were passed. No Greek could say that he lived by this or that book of laws, no matter the breadth of his literacy or the depth of his wisdom.

Matters were different in ancient Israel, where the Hebrews were guided in great detail by their Torah, which is still called *The Sepher Torah*, the Book of the Torah. This is the foundational part of the Hebrew Bible, to which is added a collection of poetic writings of the Prophets, and a third collection of even more poetic "Writings."

Thus, the *Tanach* contains some 30 individual books (the total depends on how one counts a single volume that was later split into two parts, like Samuel I and II). For more than two millennia, the Hebrews have governed themselves via a complex literature on the theme of living a just and sanctified life.

The Masoretic text of the Hebrew Bible was completed in about the year 1000, so accurate that it became the stand-ard version of the *Tanach*, pushing other versions aside as it spread in Latin and Greek throughout the ancient Levant and then into Europe.

An important, but overlooked, quality of the Masoret-ic text is that it was not simply canonized but edited with a purpose. Stories with rich literary content were particu-larly chosen, such as Samson's long-lasting struggle with the Philistines and their tempting women, David's passion for women and war, and Solomon's affair with the Queen of Sheba. Less well-crafted stories were less likely to be included, such as the Book of Gad the Seer, mentioned below in the Book of Chronicles.

Why Chronicles, a particularly uninteresting book, was canonized despite its dullness, is something of a mystery. Later divided into two parts, Chronicles is a repetitive recount of historical material that had already found a richer telling in Samuel and Kings. But there is one quality of Chronicles that may have merited its canonization, and that is its respect for literary books, as we see in 29:25-29, at the end of Part I:

And the Lord magnified Solomon exceedingly in the sight of all Israel and bestowed upon him such royal majesty as had not been on any King before him in Israel. Thus David, the son of Jesse, reigned over all Israel . . . seven years reigned he in Hebron, and thirty and three years reigned he in Jerusalem. And he died in good old age, full of days, riches, and honor: and Solomon his son reigned in his stead. Now the acts of David the king, first and last, behold they are written in the book of Samuel, and in the book of Nathan the prophet, and in the book of Gad the Seer.

The "Book of Samuel" actually tells us a much more complicated story about David than this sketch, which is, in any case, inaccurate. David did *not* die "in good old age, full of days, riches, and honor." He actually expired in a way that obliquely reminds the reader of his dishonorable womanizing, as we learn in I Kings 1-4:

> Now king David was old and stricken in years; and they covered him with clothes, but he gat no heat. Wherefore his servants said unto him, Let there be sought for my lord the king, a young virgin: and let her stand before the king, and let her cherish him, and let her lie in thy bosom, that my king may get heat. So they sought for a fair damsel throughout all the coasts of Israel, and found Abishag . . . and brought her before the king. And the damsel was very fair, and cherished the king, and ministered to him: but the king knew her not [i.e., did not have sexual relations with her].

In case we miss the allusion to David's eye for the "fair damsel," Bathsheba, the narrator reminds us that this time, with the fair Abishag in David's bed, there was no sex involved. When one is reminded not to think of sex with Bathsheba, that is actually what one does recall, especially since David's servants were careful to seek "throughout all the coasts of Israel" to find the fairest damsel in the land.

Also, of note in the conclusion to I Chronicles is a cleansing of Solomon's story. The text of 20:25-27 misrepresents the sanctity of his unwise reign while deflating the praise for his highly honored father.

> The Lord magnified Solomon exceedingly in the sight of all Israel and bestowed upon him such

majesty as had not been on any King before him in Israel."

This passage implies that the reign of David was less glorious than that of Solomon. But have we not seen that both celebrated kings were not as glorious as they were supposed to be? Thus, the Book of Chronicle in this one instance can be valued, not for its plodding repetition of history recorded elsewhere, but for challenging its readers to read more carefully, a necessary requirement for those who follow ethical monotheism.

The Book of Maccabees (later divided into two) was not canonized, not because it was dull, but because its account of the Hebrews' military victory over Seleucid tyranny in about 168 BCE likely encouraged Bar Kochba's disastrous rebellion against Roman tyranny 300 years later. From Paul Johnson's *History of the Jews* we learn that even after the destruction of Jerusalem in 70 CE, there were still about 10 million Jews in the Roman world, about half of whom lived in Israel.

During their first destruction of Jerusalem, the Romans concentrated on slaughtering the troublesome Jews in their homeland, but after the Bar-Kochba rebellion in about 135 CE, the Roman sword was supplemented by legions of rulers who wished to prove their loyalty to Rome, or to avenge the Jews' killing of their new god, Christ, the Lord. By 500 CE the remnant of Israel consisted of about a half-million souls, living mainly around Lyon, France, where the family of Herod and his court had fled. Thus, after Bar Kochba the Jews lost 95% of their people, by far the worst catastrophe in their long history of suffering the consequences of their irrational behavior.

In the edited Masoretic texts we find an organic whole, a portrayal of the central aspects of the Hebrews' national life, their recurrent propensity to undermine their own monotheistic values, and their impressive creativity that sometimes helped mitigate disasters like the destruction of Jerusalem and its inhabitants twice.

To follow the *Tanach*'s weave of laws, histories, and stories requires more than a superficial understanding of the mind. What is needed is a psychology that can integrate Eve's sophism, Cain's impulsive fratricide, Korach's hyper-intense populism, Saul's paranoia, David's manic-depression, Samson's erratic executive function, and Solomon's shaky wisdom. With an understanding of such a psychology, the children of Israel might have avoided the failures of their stiff-necked forefathers, as well as their exile to Babylonia. But they did come close to producing such a psychology.

The fragility of the Children of Israel's mastery of monotheism takes center stage in the *Tanach*. From the conquest of the Land to the culminating destruction of Jerusalem in 586 BCE, they could not reliably muster the mental capacity required by ethical monotheism. And so they were exiled, unable to protect themselves from their own inadequate minds. Yes, they failed to follow their Lord's commandments, but more importantly, they never quite developed the mental capacity to do so.

Nevertheless, the history of the Hebrews also demonstrates their redemptive creativity, their literate capacity to weave in their minds an acceptance of a civilizing law decreed by an invisible God.

One can think of Hebrews' prayer shawl, or *tallit*, as the emblem of that weave, for that is the way it is described in Numbers 15:37-41:

> And the Lord spake unto Moses, saying, Speak unto the children of Israel, and bid them that they make them fringes in the borders of their garments throughout their generations, and that they put on the fringe of the borders a ribbon of blue . . . that ye may look upon it, and remember all the commandments of the Lord, and do them; and that ye seek not after your own heart [i.e., your own mind] and your own eyes [your own misguided perception] after which ye use to go a whoring: that ye may remember and do all my commandments and be holy unto your God. I am the Lord your God which brought you out of the Land of Egypt.

We see here that it takes a good deal of cognitive capacity to fashion a *tallit*, to recall the Exodus from Egypt, to understand the reference to "all the commandments," and to live accordingly. Perhaps there is no better summary of the mindset required of a righteous Hebrew than this passage about the making of a prayer shawl. What is valued here is the ability to weave into the mind abstract ideas woven into cloth, a weave of Bible, literacy, and mind.

Thus, the requirement to weave and wear a *tallit* was designed to enhance the Hebrews' perception ("your own eyes") and their minds ("your own heart"). This might keep them from returning to the slavery to their appetites, and from forgetting that they were lifted out of slavery in Egypt to be "holy" (*kadosh*).

But what does "holy" mean? To Jews *kadosh* means that which is replete with Hebraic values, like those carefully set forth in the *Tanach*. But how the brain develops a sense of value has remained, despite the efforts by neuroscientists and philosophers, insufficiently elucidated. Even today it remains unknown whether a yet-undiscovered theory of mind might improve the *Tanach*'s understanding of how to overcome psychological impediments and create a just society.

The Craft of Cain
Victor M. Erlich, 1964

CPSIA information can be obtained
at www.ICGtesting.com
Printed in the USA
BVHW022244280522
638400BV00018B/763